Auditor Pocket Guide

Process Auditing to ISO/TS 16949:2002

Also available from ASQ Quality Press:

ISO/TS 16949:2002: Quality Systems—Automotive Suppliers—Particular Requirements for the Application of ISO 9001:2000
ISO/TS

Integrating QS-9000 with Your Automotive Quality System,
Third Edition
D. H. Stamatis

Six Sigma for the Office: A Pocket Guide
Roderick A. Munro

Failure Mode and Effect Analysis: FMEA from Theory to Execution, Second Edition
D. H. Stamatis

Six Sigma for the Shop Floor: A Pocket Guide
Roderick A. Munro

ASQ Pocket Guides—
Buy in Quantity for Special Discounts!

Automotive Internal Auditor Pocket Guide

Process Auditing to
ISO/TS 16949:2002

Roderick A. Munro

ASQ Quality Press
Milwaukee, Wisconsin

American Society for Quality, Quality Press, Milwaukee 53203
© 2004 by ASQ
All rights reserved. Published 2004
Printed in the United States of America

12 11 10 09 08 07 06 05 04   5 4 3 2

Library of Congress Cataloging-in-Publication Data

Munro, Roderick A.
  Automotive internal auditor pocket guide : process auditing to ISO/TS
16949:2002 / Roderick A. Munro.
    p. cm.
  Includes bibliographical references and index.
  ISBN 0-87389-617-3 (soft cover, spiral bound : alk. paper)
  1. Automobile industry and trade—Quality control—Standards—
Handbooks, manuals, etc. 2. Automobile industry and trade—
Auditing—Standards—Handbooks, manuals, etc. I. Title.

  TL278.5.M86 2004
  338.4'7629222'0685—dc22   2004002513

Publisher: William A. Tony
Acquisitions Editor: Annemieke Hytinen
Project Editor: Paul O'Mara
Production Administrator: Randall Benson
Special Marketing Representative: Matt Meinholz

ASQ Mission: The American Society for Quality advances individual,
organizational, and community excellence worldwide through learning,
quality improvement, and knowledge exchange.

Attention Bookstores, Wholesalers, Schools, and Corporations: ASQ Quality
Press books, videotapes, audiotapes, and software are available at quantity
discounts with bulk purchases for business, educational, or instructional use.
For information, please contact ASQ Quality Press at 800-248-1946, or write to
ASQ Quality Press, P.O. Box 3005, Milwaukee, WI 53201-3005.

To place orders or to request a free copy of the ASQ Quality Press Publications
Catalog, including ASQ membership information, call 800-248-1946. Visit our
Web site at www.asq.org or http://qualitypress.asq.org.

∞ Printed on acid-free paper

To my mother, Georgina Antoniette Munro, who left this plane of existence during the final stages of this book. Although she did not see this work completed, she promised to be with me always.

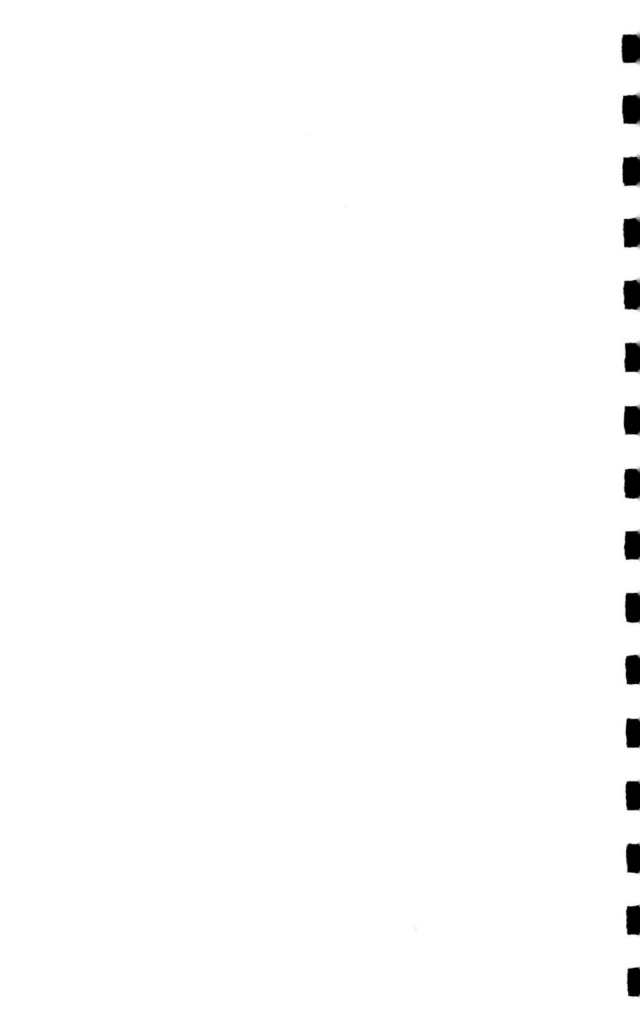

Contents

Preface

Welcome to the *Automotive Internal Auditor Pocket Guide*. This book is designed as a reference manual for conducting internal audits to ISO/TS 16949:2002 using the new process approach. It does not cover all the aspects of how to conduct internal audits, as there are many training programs and books available that cover the procedures of internal auditing in depth. This pocket manual is designed to help and assist internal auditors planning and performing process audits with ideas, tips, suggestions, and so on, to become more effective as an auditor and satisfy the audit customers (top management, auditees, and external customers).

The ISO/TS 16949:2002 standard requires more participation on the part of everyone in the organization and requires top management to be directly involved with the auditing process. Another keynote that will be discussed is the need to identify customers (internal and external) for the various processes and to collect tangible data on customer satisfaction.

This book is a continuation of a series of works started by the author referred to as QUIT— "Quality in Training." It is hoped that through this ongoing series people will be helped in finding joy in the work that they do, leading to healthier, happier lives.

In the Zen Buddhist text *The Art of Living,* it states:

> The Master in the art of living makes little distinction between his work and his play, his labor and his leisure, his mind his body, his education and his recreation, his love and his religion. He hardly knows which is which. He simply pursues his vision of excellence in whatever he does, leaving others to decide whether he is working or playing. To him he is always doing both.

Acknowledgments

A lthough some people have asked for a complete reference guide for automotive internal
auditors, it was felt that a pocket guide to high-
light some of the more important items would be
more useful to those who are on the floor doing
internal audits. To this end, this book has been
developed from comments and suggestions of
hundreds of participants in classes dealing with
automotive internal auditing. I would like to
thank all of them and a number of instructors
who have worked with the author to discuss areas
for continual improvement in internal auditing,
including David Lusk, Joe Kausek, George Moura-
dian, Norma Simons, and Dr. Dean Stamatis.

I would also like to thank ASQ Quality Press
for their time and efforts to help this pocket guide
become a reality. Especially Annemieke Hytinen,
Acquisitions Editor, and Paul O'Mara, Project
Editor. Their help has been most valuable in

ensuring that this pocket guide will be useful to automotive internal auditors.

Finally, a personal thank-you to Dr. Elizabeth J. Rice-Munro, who spent countless hours coaching me and saying "shut off that TV" to help ensure that this product was produced.

1

History of
Automotive Auditing

The automotive industry has been actively auditing suppliers for more than 40 years, but the history of auditing goes back centuries. The focus of this book will be current practice for the process approach to the ISO/TS 16949:2002 and its related support documents (core tools, customer specific requirements, rules, guidelines, and so on). The auditor would do well to have a basic understanding of how the current auditing system came to be and what is expected in the automotive industry.

MILITARY STANDARD 8959

During World War II, the entire manufacturing component of industry turned to the war effort. People who had never seen the inside of manufacturing plants were brought in to replace the men who went off to fight. With the loss of skilled works, many techniques were developed to assist in ensuring that product was the best that it could be for the men on the front lines. During this time, the U.S. government was looking for a way to ensure that suppliers delivered consistently good quality parts. A practice of auditing was developed and was combined in 1956 in the first Military (Mil) Specification (Std) 8959 (Marash, Berman, and Flynn 2003).

SPEAR AND Q-101

The automotive industry came under the Mil-Std 8959A and also wanted to monitor suppliers. Ford Motor Company (Ford) and General Motors Corporation (GM) started officially auditing suppliers in 1964 with the release of their standards Q-101 and Supplier Performance and Evaluation Report (SPEAR), respectively. Chrysler Corporation and American Motors followed a few years later with their own versions of the programs.

During the late 1960s and throughout the 1970s, the automotive industry developed the practice of conducting yearly audits on suppliers differently from other industries' auditing practices (for example, aerospace and nuclear fields). In the automotive industry, the common practice was to have supplier quality assurance (SQA) auditors spend one day reviewing each plant regardless of how large the operation was. This sometimes left time for the auditor to conduct only a bench audit. Other auditors may have found themselves being distracted by suppliers who had things they wanted to hide from the customer.

Simultaneously, in Europe auditing of suppliers was becoming widespread. The English especially moved forward with their British Standard (BS) 5750, which became a national standard used by many organizations from schools and hospitals to manufacturing plants. It was this standard that the International Organization for Standardization (ISO) used as the first draft of ISO 9001:1987.

PENTASTAR, Q-1, AND TARGETS FOR EXCELLENCE

Back in the United States, the automotive original equipment manufacturers (OEMs) were being challenged to coordinate some of the multiple demands being put on suppliers. In the late 1970s, Chrysler, Ford, and GM (the Big Three)—along with a number of suppliers—formed a not-for-profit organization to work on standards to be used in the U.S. automotive industry. This group was called the Automotive Industry Action Group (AIAG) and was based in Southfield, Michigan.

The first task that the AIAG worked on was to standardize how bar coding (a new technology at that time for labeling shipping containers) would be used in the industry. Up to that point, it appeared as if each of the Big Three would have to develop separate technologies, which would have caused a profound mess for suppliers.

Then in 1979, the National Broadcasting Company (NBC) aired a show narrated by Lloyd Dobyns called "If Japan Can . . . Why Can't We." It originally aired very late at night, but some executives from both Ford and GM saw the show. They became very curious about someone named Dr. W. Edwards Deming and wanted to know more about what he had taught the Japanese. Remember that the perception was, at that time, that the Japanese had taken the U.S. automotive industry by storm in the mid to late 1970s! Each company requested that NBC rebroadcast the show during prime time and circulated memos within each company directing that employees should watch the program. Many did, and Deming started visiting both Ford and GM.

It was during this time (early 1980s) that the big three started developing their award programs. Ford started its Q1 Award (which is different from the Q-101 supplier survey, Ford thus having two processes) around 1981; GM followed by replacing it's SPEAR audits with the Target for Excellence Award, and Chrysler developed the Pentastar

Award. The SQA at each company worked with the purchasing departments to monitor suppliers and grant awards to those who could meet the high levels established by each company.

The rate of quality improvement increased greatly in the United States during the mid to late 1980s. Ford even used a new group called Supplier Quality Improvement (SQI) to work with suppliers in the earliest phases of programs. This initiative proved so effective at preventing issues at launch that it was integrated with the SQA in 1995 to create the Supplier Technical Assistant (STA), which is used today. During the early 1990s at least one leading bank tried to benchmark Ford's Q1 program to understand what the automotive industry was doing to make such great improvements.

AUTOMOTIVE CORE TOOLS

One of Deming's first requests of the two automotive giants was that they should set up vigorous training programs for suppliers based on quality. This request led to each company developing and requiring training by company employees and suppliers in statistical process control (SPC). By the late 1980s, suppliers were requesting that this process be standardized. Thus, AIAG was given the task to start work on standardizing quality-related tools. The first manual to come out was *Measurement Systems Analysis* (MSA) in 1990 followed by *Statistical Process Control* in 1992. The same team had worked on both books and the AIAG realized that to create more books, they would need more development teams. Thus, three more projects were started, which resulted in: *Production Part Approval Process* (PPAP) in 1993, *Failure Mode and Effects Analysis* (FMEA) in 1993, and *Advance Product Quality Planning and Control Plans* (APQP) in 1994. Three of the manuals were updated in 1995: MSA, PPAP, and FMEA. Today these five books make up the core quality tools that are required in the U.S. automotive industry. At the time of this writing, the current editions included: SPC 1992, APQP 1994, PPAP (3rd) 1999, FMEA (3rd) 2001, and MSA (3rd) 2002. You may want to check the AIAG Web site at www.aiag.org to ensure that you have the most recent copy available.

QS-9000: 1994, 1996, 1998

With the worldwide release of the ISO 9000 Series in 1987, and the United States effort to commonize standards starting with the MSA in 1990 and SPC in 1992, a call came out from suppliers (during a joint conference sponsored by the AIAG and American Society for Quality [ASQ] Automotive Division) to standardize the OEM audit programs. Executives of the automotive industry and AIAG started looking at this possibility, and the Supplier Quality Requirements Task Force (SQRTF) was given the task to combine the three programs, Chrysler's Pentastar, Ford's Q-101, and GM's Targets for Excellence, into one program. The first draft was called Quality System Requirements and was circulated for internal OEM review in early 1994. It was renamed Quality Systems Requirements QS-9000 and released in August of 1994. It used the same auditing scheme as ISO 9001:1994 (also having just been updated) and registrars (third-party independent organizations controlled by appointed groups through ISO) began auditing suppliers to the new automotive standard.

The use of ISO 9001:1994 for industry-specific standards was quickly adopted by other groups (aerospace, telecommunications, and others). The European automotive community also started developing individual standards based on the ISO requirements for their suppliers.

ISO/TS 16949:1999, 2002

The next challenge was for the global automotive industry to devise one standard to replace the variety of national standards. How about developing a single global standard under the ISO that went beyond the requirements of ISO 9001:1994 that was specific to the industry? The United States and European automotive manufacturers developed the International Automotive Task Force (IATF). This group started working toward a commonized U.S./Europe standard. Membership in IATF included: BMW, DaimlerChrysler, Fiat, Ford Motor Company, General Motors (including Opel Vauxhall), PSA Peugeot-Citroen, Renault SA, and Volkswagen along with respective trade associations—AIAG (U.S.), ANFIA (Italy), FIEV (France), SMMT (U.K.), and VDA (Germany).

Up to this point the ISO had resisted developing industry-specific standards and wanted to stay with general standards for global applications. However, given the size of the worldwide automotive industry, the ISO gave in to this request and the first ISO technical specification (TS) 16949 came out in 1999. This standard was based primarily on the QS-9000 and the German VDA 6. An oversight board was created to be a link between ISO and the IATF, which was called the International Automotive Oversight Bureau (IAOB). It is this group that approves registrars for the 16949 standard. The next release of the ISO 9000 series occurred in 2000, and the IAOB started on the next revision of the 16949, which was released in 2002.

In reference to ISO/TS 16949:2002, the ISO states: "The document is a common automotive quality system requirements catalog based on ISO 9001:2000, AVSQ (Italian), EAQF (French), QS-9000 (U.S.), and VDA6.1 (German) automotive catalogs. This document, coupled with customer-specific requirements, defines quality system requirements for use in the automotive supply chain."

The IATF oversees 16949, the number ISO has given to the global automotive community for their work. In working with the standard and the registration process:

> . . . the IATF has developed a common registration scheme for supplier third-party registration to the ISO/TS 16949. The registration scheme includes third-party auditor qualifications and common rules for consistent global registration. Some of the benefits of the IATF registration scheme include:
>
> - Improved product and process quality
>
> - Additional confidence for global sourcing
>
> - Reassignment of supplier resources to quality improvement

- Common quality system approach in the supply chain for supplier/subcontractor development and consistency

- Reduction in multiple third-party registrations.

WHAT'S NEXT

The next challenge that faces the IAOB is to get truly global acceptance of 16949. Up to this point, it has been primarily the United States and Europe that use 16949 widely. The Japanese have agreed in principle, but have not gone so far as requiring suppliers to register. Also, you may notice that the standard's full title is ISO/TS 16949:2002. The "TS" stands for *technical specification* and under ISO rules is only good for three years with one extension. Thus, with the first release in 1999 and the second in 2002, the year 2005 will become an important year, as we will be looking at another possible update of ISO 9001 and the full status of ISO 16949. If the IAOB does not gain full agreement by all the automotive OEMs by that time, then there is a possibility that 16949 could be withdrawn and we could be facing a return to each OEM requiring its own program for supplier qualifications worldwide!

INTERNAL AUDITOR RESPONSIBILITY

As an internal auditor, you should be aware of the status of the standards so you can talk about what is current if requested by your management or an external auditor. The primary Web sites to help you stay updated include: www.aiag.org, www.iaob.org (it has been suggested that this site be visited weekly) and www.iso.ch/iso/en/ISOOnline. openerpage.

While using this pocket guide, the internal auditor should take note of the following:

- Top management should be using the eight quality management system principles to manage the organization.

- ISO/TS 16949:2002 certificates that are issued by registrars are site specific. However, if you are part of a larger company and one of the other certificates "goes down," then your plant will lose its certificate as well.

- The U.S. and European OEMs all use the ISO/TS 16949:2002 standard, but in Europe, things are done slightly differently, which this book does not cover.

- IAOB has identified the top six witness audit issues raised in the United States as:
  - Readiness review incomplete (by top management).
  - Not auditing to the process approach.
  - Lack of auditing either the customer-specific requirements or core tool. (Note: the customer-specific requirements will soon include the major tier-one organizations, which are being planned to be found at www.aiag.org.)
  - Failure to audit all levels/activities of the organization.
  - Failure to audit all shifts in operation.
  - Failure to write clear, complete findings.
- Process identification.
- Customer identification.

SUMMARY

All processes must have an output; otherwise, they need to be eliminated as waste! Thus, the person(s) who receives the output of a process can be called the customer(s). So, customers can be internal to your plant or external. They could also be identified as the person(s) who will ultimately use your product in some final assembly that they buy for personal use. These customers could be anyone who receives reports, parts, services, or anything else a process may deliver. It is expected in the ISO/TS 16949:2002 standard that data will be collected on how well the customers are satisfied with the outputs of the process. Thus, top management will need to identify the key processes (using both macro and micro process maps) to identify which customers data will be sought from to compile a satisfaction measurement. These customer satisfaction measures are to be collected on an ongoing basis and correlated with existing process measures with the intent of showing continual improvement over time.

2

Automotive Internal Auditor Qualifications and Background Information

Automotive internal auditors have a need to upgrade their auditing skills to meet the ISO/TS 16949:2002 and related requirements. We have moved from element-based auditing to process approach–based auditing (discussed in chapter 3). This means that auditors need to ask questions differently and look at things differently. How do you audit in the absence of a documented procedure? Internal auditors will be looking at the results of the process and how the process is operating (meeting the objectives) in what we call the process approach.

The foundations for these changes can be found in a number of documents that are associated with ISO/TS 16949:2002. This chapter reviews the basics of the various groups now involved with the automotive standard, the various related documents, and the automotive internal auditor qualifications and what the auditor will need to do to stay current with the standard.

Note: In all cases, the most current documents at the time of the printing of this pocket guide have been used. Users should check identified Web sites for updates, as the automotive industry is constantly updating requirements. It has been suggested that this is a good thing, for if the OEMs did not update the materials, then that would be a sign that they did not feel that the information was important!

ISO 19011:2002 (BSR/ISO/ASQ Q19011-2002) GUIDELINES FOR QUALITY AND/OR ENVIRONMENT MANAGEMENT SYSTEM AUDITING

It is expected that the internal auditing program will be conducted to the 19011 requirements. There are four basic clauses that top management must address in selecting auditors and maintaining an effective audit program:

- *Clause 4: Principles of audit program.*
  The internal auditors need to be ethical, be able to provide fair (as in appropriate) assessments, show a level of professionalism as defined by the management, be independent of the work that they do

normally, and have been trained in evidence-based process approach auditing.

- *Clause 5: General.* The audit program is to be managed with identified objectives and goals. Responsibilities, resources, and procedures are to be clearly defined and implemented with records maintained, reviewed, and acted upon accordingly (as noted in the standard).

- *Clause 6: Audit activities.* The audit process should follow a clearly defined process and apply all the basics of good auditing practice and techniques (as flowcharted and outlined in the standard).

- *Clause 7: Competence and evaluation of auditors.* Management must choose internal auditors who are competent in conducting internal audits. The standard has lists of items to be considered for personal attributes; knowledge and skills; education, work experience, auditor training, and auditor experience; maintenance and improvement of competence and how auditor should be evaluated.

The standard defines an audit as a systematic, independent, and documented process for obtaining records, statements of fact, or other information that is relevant to the set of policies, procedures, or requirements and verifiable, and evaluating it objectively to determine the extent to which the set of polices, procedures, or requirements are fulfilled.

INTERNAL AUDITOR SELECTION

Management will need to develop their internal auditor qualification guidelines based on several documents. The primary documents include ISO 19011 and the Ford Motor Company Customer-Specific Requirements. (Although the latter is for Ford suppliers specifically, at the time of this manual's printing discussions are ongoing about making this an automotive industrywide requirement.) Management must use the internal audit program to provide inputs into the management review process, so they should be very selective in choosing personnel to be internal auditors. They need to be very good people that management can rely on to help ensure that the internal audit program is a value-added process within the organization.

Generally speaking, automotive internal auditors should have either of the following qualifications:

- Be formally trained as an ISO/TS 16949:2002 internal auditor.

- Meet some minimum number of audit days in an on-the-job audit process led by internal auditors who have formal training.

Formal internal auditor training to ISO/TS 16949:2002 usually covers the following:

- An initial assessment of the understanding and ability to utilize the standard followed by formal training (usually one-day minimum):

  - The technical specification ISO/TS 16949:2002

  - Related core tools (for example, APQP, PPAP, FMEA, SPC, and MSA)

  - Applicable customer-specific requirements

  - The automotive process approach to auditing

- Ongoing testing and training to understand and apply (usually one-day minimum):

  - The technical specification ISO/TS 16949:2002

  - Related core tools (for example, APQP, PPAP, FMEA, SPC, and MSA)

  - Applicable customer-specific requirements

- The automotive process approach to auditing

- Conducts practice sessions equivalent to one audit day in:

  - Case study audits, and/or

  - Auditing role plays/simulations, and/or

  - On-site audits

Most programs will require that instructors who have met lead auditor qualification (not necessarily RAB or IRCA lead auditors) and who have auditing experience conduct the internal auditor training.

INTERNATIONAL AUTOMOTIVE TASK FORCE

Under QS-9000, there is the SQRTF. The International Automotive Task Force (IATF) includes the SQRTF and representatives from the European automotive industry, along with the respective trade associations, to form an "ad hoc" group of automotive manufacturers. This group is responsible for developing consensus regarding the international fundamental quality system requirements. They are also responsible for developing policies and procedures for registrars to follow and maintaining a list of qualified registrars to the ISO/TS 16949:2002.

The current IATF members include the following vehicle manufacturers: BMW, Daimler-Chrysler, Fiat, Ford Motor Company, General Motors (including Opel and Vauxhall), PSA Peugeot-Citroen, Renault SA, Volkswagen, and their respective trade associations—AIAG (U.S.), ANFIA (Italy), FIEV (France), SMMT (U.K.), and VDA (Germany).

INTERNATIONAL AUTOMOTIVE OVERSIGHT BUREAU

The International Automotive Oversight Bureau (IAOB) is an IATF oversight office. The IAOB is a Michigan corporation; members include DaimlerChrysler, Ford Motor Company, General Motors, and AIAG.

The IAOB was established to:

- Implement and manage the ISO/TS 16949 registration scheme oversight activities on behalf of the IATF.

- Manage and coordinate with the IATF European Oversight Office to ensure global consistency of the ISO/TS 16949 registration scheme.

- Support the IATF in the pursuit of global harmonization with other automotive manufacturers.

- Develop and maintain a central IATF database of strategic information to assist in the management of the registration scheme.

AUTOMOTIVE CERTIFICATION SCHEME FOR ISO/TS 16949:2002— RULES FOR ACHIEVING IATF RECOGNITION

Although specifically aimed at the registrars and external auditors, this 25-page manual expects that the top management at your plant will follow the same basic auditing guidelines for the internal auditing program (Annex 1 Rules for auditing management systems according to ISO/TS 16949:2002—an eight-page flowchart). The rules book contains six sections covering: certification body, audit process, audit team, other requirements, ISO/TS 16949:2002 certificate content requirements, and forms and tables. Registrars (who are qualified to conduct ISO/TS 16949:2002 audits) have a number of "shall" statements that they must comply with.

In section 2, two definitions are given that will be important to internal auditors (quoted):

2.8 A major nonconformity is one or more of:

- The absence of or total breakdown of a system to meet an ISO/TS 16949:2002 requirement. A number of minor nonconformities against one requirement can represent a total breakdown of the system and thus be considered a major nonconformity.

- Any noncompliance that would result in the probable shipment of nonconforming product. A condition that may result in the failure or materially reduce the usability of the products or services for their intended purpose.

- A noncompliance that judgment and experience indicate is likely either to result in the failure of the quality management system or to materially reduce its ability to assure controlled processes and products.

A minor nonconformity is a failure to comply with ISO/TS 16949:2002, which based on judgment and experience, is not likely to result in the failure of the quality management system or reduce its ability to assure controlled processes or products. It may be one of the following:

- A failure in some part of the organization's documented quality management system relative to ISO/TS 16949:2002

- A single observed lapse in following one item of a company's quality management system

There are a number of items in the "rules" that registrars and external auditors must comply with. Internal auditors should use this as a general guideline and be aware of what registrars will want before and during their audit process.

IATF GUIDANCE TO ISO/TS 16949:2002

The guidance document is for both registrars and internal audit programs in supplier plants. It is designed to clarify clauses in ISO/TS 16949:2002, similar to what the Sanctioned Interpretations did for QS-9000. As the internal auditor is creating specific checklists for use in your plant, you will need to review this document for applicable explanations to areas you might be auditing.

QUALITY SYSTEM ASSESSMENT CHECKLIST—CHECKLIST TO ISO/TS 16949:2002

This document replaces the Quality System Assessment (QSA) used by QS-9000. It is a complete general checklist to ISO/TS 16949:2002 to help internal auditors ensure that the entire requirement is covered during the internal audit. As the internal auditor is creating specific checklists for use in your plant, you will also need to review this document for general requirements and make specific notes for your plant. Chapter 3 is designed to assist the internal auditor in using the standard, guidance, and checklist to create a plant-specific checklist.

CUSTOMER-SPECIFIC REQUIREMENTS (DATED MATERIALS)

The most current customer-specific requirements can be found on the Web at www.iaob.org/. Since these can be changed at any time by the OEM, it is recommended that your plant check the Web site regularly to ensure that you have the most current requirements. Each company has specific areas that it wants that go beyond what is called out in the other documents relating to ISO/TS 16949:2002. If your plant supplies any of these companies, then the internal audit program must include the items found in these requirements as part of your internal audit.

Some of the specific items found in these documents include:

- DaimlerChrysler (Chrysler Group) Customer-Specific Requirements—For Use with ISO/TS 16949 Second Edition—September 2003

  - To ensure continuing conformance to all DaimlerChrysler requirements, a complete annual layout inspection, including all subcomponents, shall be required for all parts.

  - Continuing conformance inspection/tests shall be performed during the model year to assure production items or products continue to meet specified requirements and tolerances.

  - An organization shall have at least two individuals at each of its locations that have completed all DaimlerChrysler Corporation PRISM training.

- Ford Motor Company Customer-Specific Requirements—For Use with ISO/TS 16949:2002—October 2003

- Management review input must also include the Q1 2002 Manufacturing Site Assessment results (see requirement for Web site locations of listed references).

- The organization shall ensure that only trained and qualified personnel are involved in all aspects of the manufacture or design (as appropriate) of Ford Motor Company parts.

- Setup verification requirements include manual tooling exchanges. Records of all setup verifications shall be maintained for one year.

- All gages used for checking Ford components/parts per the control plan shall have a gage R&R performed in accordance with the appropriate methods described by the latest AIAG *Measurement Systems Analysis Manual* (MSA) to determine measurement capability. (Note that his would mean using "K" values aligned with six sigma.)

- Internal quality management system auditors shall be qualified per 4.39.1 or 4.39.2 (as discussed earlier in this chapter).

- GM Customer Specifics—ISO/TS 16949—
  September 2002

  - GM supply organizations shall verify
    annually that they are using the latest
    version of these documents:

    * Pre-Production/Pilot Material
      Shipping Procedures (GM 1407)

    * Supplier Submission of Match Check
      Material (GM 1689)

    * Shipping Parts Identification Label
      Standard (GM 1724)

    * Component Verification & Traceability
      Procedure (GM 1730)

    * Traceability Identifier Equipment
      (TIR 15-300) (GM 1731)

    * Specifications for Part and Component
      Bar Codes ECV/VCVS (GM 1737)

    * Supplier Quality Processes and
      Measurements Procedure (GM 1746)

    * Continuous Improvement Procedure
      (GM 1747)

    * GP-10 Evaluation and Accreditation
      Test Facilities (GM 1796/A)

* Shipping and Delivery Performance Requirements (GM 1797)

* Key Characteristics Designation System (KCDS) (GM 1805 QN)

* General Procedure for Pre-Prototype and Prototype Material (GM 1820)

* C4 Technology Program, GM—Supplier C4 Information (GM 1825)

* GP-12 Early Production Containment Procedure (GM 1920)

* Run at Rate Procedure (GM 1960)

SUMMARY

The internal auditor should be selected as being a person who can keep a lot of information organized and coordinated during the internal audit process. He or she will need to have good interpersonal skills to work with auditees and management, good questioning skills to conduct the process audit, good writing skills to complete reports, and good follow-up skills to ensure that corrective action reports (CARs) and preventive action reports (PARs) are closed in a timely fashion. Top management is responsible for ensuring that the internal audit program is effective and provides value-added information to the organization.

If ISO/TS 16949:2002 is costing your company money (versus saving you money), then you are doing something wrong!

3

Introduction to Process Auditing

ISO/TS 16949:2002 will require a shift in thinking for internal auditors on how they view the process and how they ask questions of the management and other people in the plant. The basic idea of process auditing is to identify the management process being utilized via the process inputs, activity, and process outputs (turtle diagram). The old way of "say what you do—do what you say—and prove it" will no longer work!

ELEMENT AUDITING

The original intent of ISO 9001:1987 was to conduct auditing in alignment with the 20 elements of the standard. This meant that under each element (such as 4.18—training), a sampling of the actual practice or records would be reviewed for conformance to the policies and procedures of the organization. This process was quickly revised in the automotive industry as the original intent of the ISO 9001:1987 standard was not as efficient as working through the various departments within the subcontractor (supplier) sequentially.

The element-based auditing approach from ISO 9001:1987 was carried forward with ISO 9001:1994 and into the Automotive Quality System Requirements QS-9000. Given the modifications of the automotive industry, under element-based auditing, internal auditors would still follow the audit approach of reviewing actual procedures being accomplished and records of such actions to ensure conformance to policies and procedures.

Thus, an internal auditor, upon entering an area (or just before), would first review the policy, procedures, FMEA, control plans, and work instructions to ensure that the work was being done according to plan. If discrepancies were found, CARs would be written against the area or department that caused the issues. This sometimes led to finger-pointing as internal auditors sometimes reported these issues only to the immediate department that they were auditing, but the concerns arose due to other groups or linkage between departments within the plant.

PROCESS AUDITING

Under ISO 9001:2000 and ISO/TS 16949:2002, the element-based approach to auditing has been changed to what is being called a process auditing approach. The practice of the automotive industry to review the entire standard as appropriate in each area visited will be continued with the additional change in focus that the auditor will start the audit with a review of the process output(s) and customer satisfaction information first and work back into the process to see what is being done to ensure or enhance customer satisfaction. Questions will change from whether you (the auditee) are following the procedures to "how is what you (the auditee) are doing ensuring that customers will be satisfied?" Thus, the idea of only following what a procedure says is no longer appropriate if that procedure does not provide happy customers!

The basis of process auditing is understood in the plan–do–check–act (PDCA) model and is depicted in Figure 3.1 of ISO/TS 16949:2002 found on page 34 (some people use a PDSA model with the "S" being study). The diagram shown here (see Figure 3.2) is similar to that model with the addition of supplier input into the product realization. Internal auditors must view the processes that they review in the light of thinking how the process might be done faster, better,

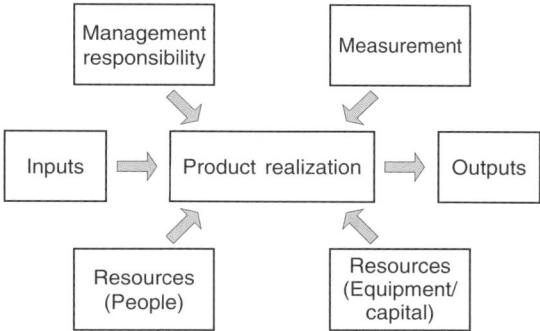

Figure 3.1   ISO/TS 16949:2002 process identification tool.

cheaper to enhance customer satisfaction versus the old way of just looking for people doing things wrong. Thus, this new auditing approach called process auditing should generate many more PARs than CARs. This new line of thinking may catch some plant managers off guard at first, but they will quickly recognize this new value-added approach to making improvements that are required within the automotive industry today. Top management, in fact, is required to use the outputs of the internal audit program to make future decisions.

Process auditing in reality turns the audit practice around 180 degrees by starting with

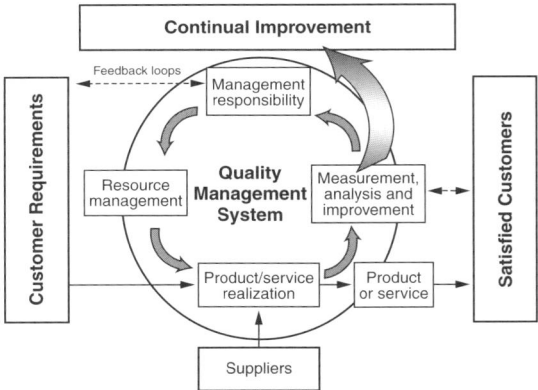

Figure 3.2 Model of a process-based QMS.
Source: Adapted from ANSI/ISO/ASQ Q9001-2000. Used with permission.

what the customer wants or needs and looking at how the process is satisfying those expectations and requirements. Internal auditors should continually be on the lookout for opportunities, identified by engineers, managers, operators, or whoever, to make things better for the customer (both internal and external). If the internal auditor's organization is to become a truly outstanding supplier in the automotive industry, these changes must occur, and the internal process auditing process becomes a key tool of management to ensure that customers' needs are being met and exceeded! Another way to say this is that the internal auditor's job is to be a reporter on innovation in the organization.

ISO/TS 16949:2002 0.2 describes the process approach as: "The application of a system of processes within an organization, together with the identification and interactions of these processes, and their management. . . ." It continues that the advantage to the process approach is a managerial control over the linkages between processes as well as over the processes' combination and interaction. With the method of the process approach in place, an emphasis of importance should be placed on:

- Understanding and meeting requirements

- The need to consider processes in terms of added value

- Obtaining results of process performance and effectiveness

- Continual improvement of processes based on objective measurement

Internal auditors will use these emphasis factors as starting points when reviewing the operational functions or departments.

PROCESS MAPPING

One of the key tools that internal auditors should have available to them is called a process map, or flowchart (see sample, Figure 3.3). The use of the process approach, which needs to be mapped by the organization, is outlined in ISO/TS 16949:2002 in section 0.2 starting on page ix. Many registrars are quickly moving toward requiring organizations to have well-defined, updated process maps for use during the registration audit. Internal auditors should also be using these within the internal audit program.

Versions of process maps are probably currently being used by various departments (maintenance,

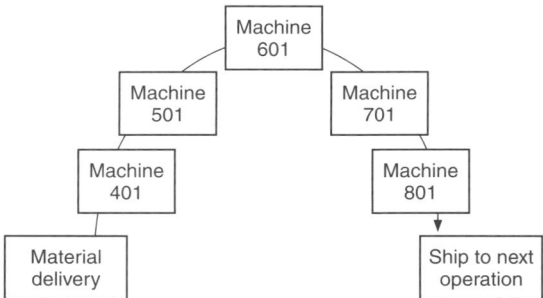

Figure 3.3 Sample process map—machine cell XYZ.

engineering, safety, environmental, supervisors, and so on) and that can present a challenge as to what map is the most current and to questions of why so many potentially different maps are being used for a given area of the plant. The differences found in these maps can lead to important findings by the auditors as to some of the reasons that things may not always work the way plans say they should.

If the internal auditor does not find any process maps (for products or information), then they (the internal auditors) will need to create them for the process. This takes time, and depending on the complexity, the activity may change multiple times during a cycle of audits conducted on the area over a year or so. This could lead to questions of lack of constancy (clause 7.1.b) in the process and/or an issue of operators or supervisors constantly changing the process without the use of appropriate data analysis (clause 8.1.2) of customer satisfaction.

IDENTIFYING MEASURABLES

To demonstrate customer satisfaction, many plants are starting to use information boards at the end of lines or departments to depict data that management or employees have deemed critical to customer satisfaction. Some of these boards are using data relating to SQDCME (safety, quality, delivery, cost, morale, environment). Whether information boards are used or not, top management will be held accountable for identifying (internal or external) customer-specific measurables by the registrar.

To identify measurables, an understanding of statistical analysis is required. Then, using the four basic areas of the "Model of a process-based QMS" (see Figure 3.2) including management responsibility, resource management, product realization, and measurement, analysis and improvement, management can start looking for the energy inputs that result in customer satisfaction. Internal auditors should be able to find evidence of this management planning in management minute meetings (this could almost be considered a management FMEA of the organization). If no reference is found, then a PAR should be written to management suggesting they conduct a formal review of the measurement system being used in the plant.

Another method that can be used to identify what customers want is quality function deployment (QFD). This method is typically used to convert the ultimate customer wants and needs into engineering specifications. This is accomplished by using the customer's requirements and understanding what they want and reverse engineering the customer's information into a set of measureable process parameters that will be needed to satisfy the customer.

Regardless of how your organization identifies measurables, the internal auditor will be responsible for looking for ways to improve the measurement process through the organization's PAR process. The key here will be to look at the energy inputs (resources and controls) to see if correlations exist with current output measures.

LINK POLICIES AND PROCEDURES

All processes in your organization need to derive their inputs from one or more processes' outputs and end up by giving their outputs to another process. Any item that the internal auditor investigates that has outputs that are not used by another process should be identified as a non-value-added process for management review! In the early phases of process auditing, one common area where this will be found is in various reports that float around the plant. At one time, a report may have been important, but the problem that initiated the report has long since ended, and the report is still being generated. This sometimes continues for many years!

Internal auditors should also be looking for linkage between policy and the objectives of the company and how are you going to carry out the policy. The macro process map should be aligned with the overall business objectives of the company and with customer wants and needs.

IDENTIFY INTERACTION BETWEEN PROCESSES

In addition to having the process maps, management must identify the linking of the various maps around the organization. This is most commonly displayed with the use of the octopus diagram (see chapter 4 and Figure 4.4, page 57). The point here is that linked processes should be working together to achieve a common objective. Internal auditors will need to study the process outputs leading to other process inputs to ensure that interactions are as planned by management. If unplanned interactions are occurring, then an evaluation may need to be made on whether to keep doing the current process or change it. The internal auditor would write these situations up as PARs for future management review and action.

Auditing is a process that interacts with the entire organization. Internal auditors should be looking for improvement links throughout the entire organization as it relates to the standard and the organizational goals in meeting customer satisfaction.

MAKE A JUDGMENT ABOUT SYSTEM EFFECTIVENESS

In QS-9000:1998, the term effectiveness, which occurs 13 times, is referring to how well the sytem (or QMS) is doing based on what the documented system says that it will do. In ISO/TS 16949:2002, the word effectiveness occurs 26 times and relates to how well the process (or QMS) is satisfying the customer.

A major shift in thinking has occurred with the application of the process approach in the automotive industry. Instead of just writing the process down, it now involves the need to understand how processes fit together to operate and control the organization. This is very important to supply information through the audit result for top management to understand and manage for results. Top management must have a process for management review, which now must focus on opportunities for improvement (the PAR process). Internal auditors will make observations, which are the outputs of reviewing a process; analyze the observations to develop findings; and create an overall output in the form of audit reports (oral and written).

The judgment that internal auditors will need to make is how well the customers are being satisfied by the current processes. This should come from data that the organization is collecting from the customers themselves. However, just sending out electronic, paper, or fax surveys will not be enough to gather the data needed to evaluate customer satisfaction.

Thus, many times, the internal auditors will initially need to write PARs, and in some cases CARs, to identify for management that customer data are missing for various parts of the process. One good area for collecting information is usually the shipping area. The personnel in shipping tend to talk with customer representatives on a daily basis and can usually get a sense of what the customers are experiencing in using the product. The internal auditor may have to do some digging to get the customer satisfaction data needed to complete the process audit.

SUMMARY

Processes need to be dynamic and must be flexible and changeable; just writing something down does not make for improvement. Process management requires that you use documentation to *manage* the process versus simply controlling the process. Management review is now required of the organization with the internal audit reports being one source of inputs to the review. Managers can then focus on opportunities for improvement of the process based on the customer satisfaction criteria.

4

Automotive Audit Approach

As we have been discussing, the old automotive quality management systems (for example, pre–ISO 9001:2000) were procedure driven while the new QMS (ISO/TS 16949:2002) is process and metric driven with the goal of being value and quality driven. This change in focus requires the entire organization to shift its thinking about how things are being done. The overall operation may not change much initially, but how things are planned, viewed, controlled, improved, and assessed will be different, from top management all the way down to the shop floor. Using some of the same tools as before, internal auditors will now have to rethink how audits are to be done and practice this new approach called the process approach.

The automotive audit approach under ISO/TS 16949:2002 is purposefully a manufacturing standard versus ISO 9001:2000! Thus, we want to focus on production and the value to the customer. This includes the support function within your plant that helps ensure that the product meets or exceeds what the customer wants and needs. The bottom line is that sustained improvement of customer satisfaction *must* be ongoing! Top management must be using such information as warranty reduction, elimination of supplier disruptions, significant improvement in delivery part quality, continual quality system improvement, and other metrics to demonstrate that your organization is following the intent of ISO/TS 16949:2002.

PLAN–DO–STUDY–ACT

Figure 4.1 shows the classical Deming plan–do–study–act (PDSA) model for improvement. Internal auditors will need to show not only how the company is using this model to improve, but also how they as internal auditors are using the model to make improvements in the way they are conducting audits and improving their skills as auditors.

If we take self-development as an example, we look at how the PDSA model might work. Under "plan," what does the auditor think or want to accomplish in becoming a better auditor? Questions could be asked such as: Am I aware of the process requirements of the areas I will be

Figure 4.1 Deming's PDSA.

auditing during this next year? Do I understand statistical analysis well enough to evaluate the process metrics? How might I ensure that all standards, references, and other items are current? Do I meet the requirements to be an auditor under the new process approach?, and so on. Table 4.1 lists some additional items to think about while planning the audit. It covers questions for consideration, auditing activities, organization considerations, pitfalls to avoid, and potential tools.

Next the auditor moves through the "do" phase of the PDSA. Here auditors will perform audits as assigned to them using the training and tools

Table 4.1   Audit planning.

Questions for consideration	What is the scope of the audit?
	Find all available information for the audit!
	   Are flowcharts available? If not, they
	   may need to be created.
	Who is involved and who should not
	   be involved?
	Does the procedure/policy make sense
	   within the framework of the business?
	Does the work instruction make sense?

Auditing activities	Review process using the flowcharts
	Assess situation.
	Identify the plant's process.
	List and prioritize issues.
	Define business impact.
	Review analytical tools that have
	   been applied.
	Are there open corrective-action reports
	   (CAR) for the process?
	Prepare audit plan.

Organization considerations	Does the work being done match the
	   work instructions, and so on?
	Identify opportunities for continual
	   improvement in the process.
	Is there support for corrective action,
	   if appropriate?

continued

continued

Pitfalls to avoid	Avoid yes/no questions. Am I checking myself and my environment for negative politics? Not being seen as a valuable resource. Not identifying a logical next step.
Potential tools	Flowcharts. Pareto analysis. Checklists. Process maps.

as appropriately as they know how. During the "study" phase, auditors should analyze how well their customers (auditees and top management) feel they did with the audit. The practice of professional auditing should be a learning event versus a cops and robbers chase: Were more PARs reported than CARs? Were all the processes reviewed covered thoroughly? What might be done to improve the audit next time? And so on.

Based on the answers the auditor discovers during the study phase, he or she then moves into the "act" phase where the auditor can make changes to improve his or her readiness for the next audit. Here you might choose to read books on auditing or the automotive standards, review the core tool books, conduct Web searches on any number of items related to auditing or related topics, seek additional training in areas you feel need improving (for example, listening skills, core tool application, writing, interpersonal skills, and so on), or any number of other things that might make you a better auditor.

When evaluating a process for continual improvement, the auditor will look for evidence that someone (or a group) in the process has thought through the steps as described previously. This will demonstrate a planned continual improvement effort versus a haphazard happening where things are changed (sometimes at random) and people hope that improvement will occur (sometimes this approach is called continual change).

CUSTOMER-ORIENTED PROCESS

The IAOB points out that top management must identify how they will apply customer-oriented processes (COPs) to their organization! This is not just a suggestion, but a requirement that external auditors should be looking for from the top management of the organization. These processes can encompass any process in the plant, with the starting point including items such as:

- Market analysis

- Bid/tender

- Order/request

- Product and process design

- Product and process verification/ validation

- Product production

- Delivery

- Payment

- Warranty/service

- Post-sales/customer feedback

These can be added to, combined, or moved around in any way that top management feels is appropriate to their organization, but top management must identify how what is being done impacts the external customers.

Some questions that top management should ask include: If the process is eliminated will the customer notice? Does the customer have a metric for the process? How do inputs and/or outputs directly affect the customer? Are any other processes important here as support processes?, and so on. Internal auditors should see evidence that questions such as these have been addressed by top management in addition to having process maps available to use during the audit.

One way to view this concept is through Figure 4.2, which is sometimes called the turtle diagram. The internal auditor will need to view the various process maps in the way that they are used by the organization to manage the business. The inputs and outputs to the process should be clear in the process map. The requirements for the process

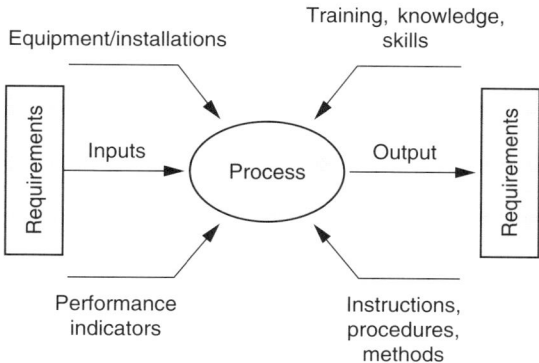

Figure 4.2 Basic turtle diagram.

inputs and outputs are to be known by all who work in that process. Think about what questions you could ask here.

Then, follow the four legs around the process. What equipment or installations are used during this process? How are these machines maintained and what type of preventive maintenance is used? What training, knowledge, or skills are needed to work in this process? Do people have the required and/or desired things needed (required may be the minimum—what is needed to continually improve)? What performance indications exist that measure the energy usage that relate to the customers measures? We want to see how SPC is being used to monitor the behavior of the process versus checking parts after they are made. What instructions, procedures, or methods are needed to maintain and improve customer satisfaction? Is the current documentation or method appropriate and working toward customer satisfaction? How do people know that they are continually improving their work toward enhancing customer satisfaction?

These questions will be built around the requirements (see chapter 3) to understand the process during the audit (see Figure 4.3). The goal of the audit should be to identify additional areas for improvement that top management can review and work toward.

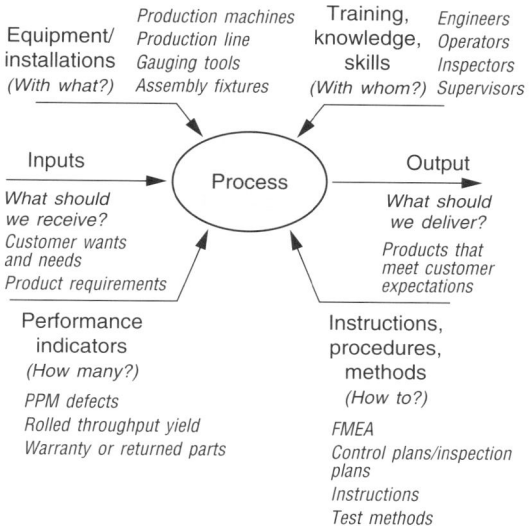

Figure 4.3 Turtle diagram explanation.

AUDIT INPUTS/OUTPUTS

The audit process itself needs to have identified inputs and outputs that will be reviewed by top management and external auditors. The basic concepts to remember when looking at a process are:

- A process owner exists.

- The process is defined.

- The process is *usually* documented.

- The linkages of the process are established.

- The process is monitored.

- Records are maintained.

Thus, the internal audit process should have its own version of the turtle diagram that will be used by the internal auditors. The legs of the turtle could include:

- Process audit approach

  - Automotive application (COP)

  - Line of sight from the organization to the customer

- Audit plan

  - Identification of key processes impacting the customer

  - Based on the processes as defined by the organization

- Performance

  - Linked to common metrics for:

    * Organization

    * Supplier

- Oversight
  - Adherence to the "rules" and common global process

The output of the audit should be an audit report that top management will use during their normally scheduled top management reviews to look for areas needing improvement within the organization. Things may need to be fixed or repaired in some cases, but if everyone in the organization is actively working on continual improvement, there should be few CARs written. As Deming, J. M. Juran, and others have pointed out, 80 percent of the things that need improvement will take top management involvement. Thus, the bulk of the audit report should be for areas needing improvement that can be addressed by top management.

THE OCTOPUS MODEL

As top management reviews the organization and internal auditors conduct the audits, there needs to be a high-level understanding of how the organization works. This is typically depicted in the *octopus model* (see Figure 4.4). This model shows that the various processes of the organization (all of the turtle diagrams) should connect to provide

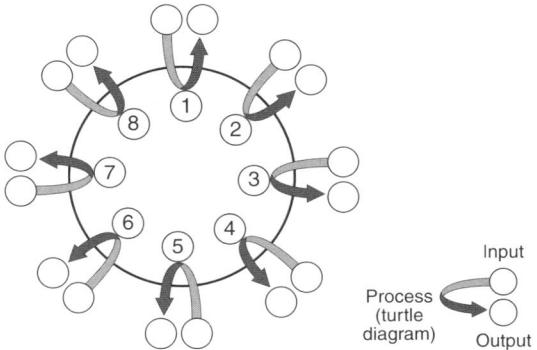

Figure 4.4   Octopus model.

the products and services that customers want and require.

The organization needs a minimum of two levels of process maps. One level will show the overall organization and how it works (octopus) and the second level will show the individual functions (purchasing, engineering, manufacturing, quality assurance, and so on). Some companies have chosen to include process maps within their procedures while others maintain separate process maps. Either way, the internal auditor will need to locate the maps and use them during the process audit process.

CRITICAL PROCESS ELEMENTS

As one of the outputs of the process audit, internal auditors should collect data on each of the processes (turtle diagrams) as they observe the processes functioning. These items can include (see Figure 4.5):

- Inputs (includes internal/external customer requirements).

- Outputs (typically includes the product but may include scrap, waste, secondary information), both expected and unexpected.

- What are the resources of the process (how is work supposed to be done)?

- What are the controls on the process (what restrictions do machines and people work under)?

- Product (this could be a design, a purchase order, a manufactured part, a service within the scope of registration—see the ISO/TS manual, and so on).

- Management responsibility (who owns the process).

- Resource management (who does what and what resources are needed).

- Product realization (the steps taken to produce/develop the product).

- Measurements (metrics) and the method of measurement (what is measured, where and how), to ensure that the product meets customer requirements—includes internally specified measurements.

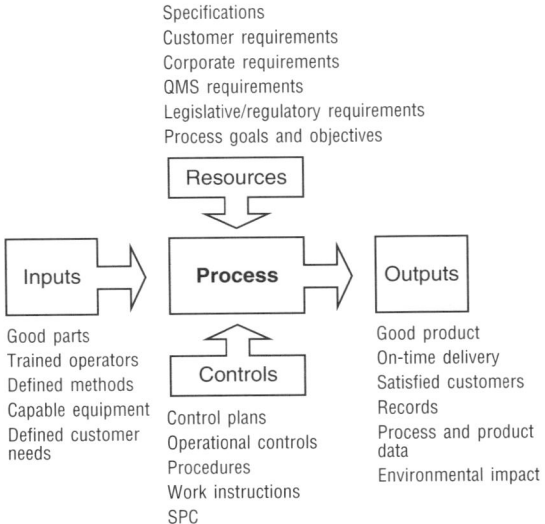

Specifications
Customer requirements
Corporate requirements
QMS requirements
Legislative/regulatory requirements
Process goals and objectives

Resources

Inputs ⟹ **Process** ⟹ Outputs

Good parts
Trained operators
Defined methods
Capable equipment
Defined customer needs

Controls

Control plans
Operational controls
Procedures
Work instructions
SPC

Good product
On-time delivery
Satisfied customers
Records
Process and product data
Environmental impact

Figure 4.5 Process auditing method.

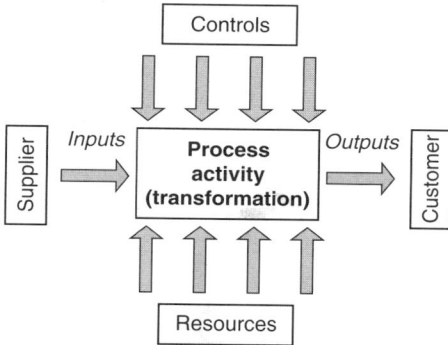

Figure 4.6   Process review.

The auditor may use any number of data collection methods (see Figures 4.6 and 4.7). However, as you collect the information, you must ensure that information is presented in the audit report to assist the top management of your organization to take appropriate action. According to the IATF Guidance to ISO/TS 16949:2002, internal auditors should include information on:

- Adequacy and accuracy of performance measurements

- Analysis of quality cost data

- Capability of processes and use of statistical techniques

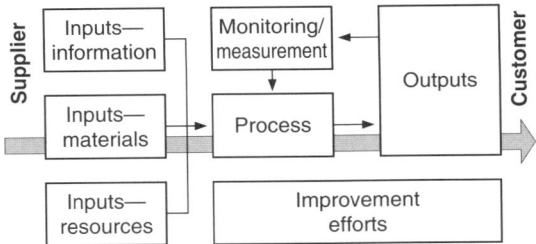

Figure 4.7 Process review.

- Effective and efficient implementation of processes

- Opportunities for continual improvement

- Process and product performance results and expectations

- Relationships with customers

SUMMARY

The organization's internal audit program will be evaluated by the registrar for continual improvement and compliance to the 19011 standard; thus, top management needs to be current on what this and the other requirements say about internal auditors. During the redesign and development of the internal auditor program to meet ISO/TS 16949:2002, top management needs to ensure that the internal audit process meets three basic areas:

- *Product.* Does everything meet requirements?

- *Manufacturing process.* Were all the proper steps followed?

- *Quality management system.* What are the process interactions and are they effective for customer satisfaction?

Since top management must address all issues prior to an external registrar coming on-site, audit plans must cover all of the organization's processes, not just clauses in the standard. This will require rigorous internal auditing prior to an external audit.

Internal auditors must use customer metrics to identify processes that are not meeting customer requirements and focus on those processes.

5

Audit Preparation

As has been discussed, internal auditing for 16949:2002 is very different than for QS-9000 or 16949:1999. In preparing for an internal audit, the primary function of the auditor in planning was to take a prepared checklist on compliance and go to the area to be audited, review the area based on the checklist, and turn in the completed paperwork (checklist, CAR, and so on).

Now, the time needed for planning for internal auditing under ISO/TS 16949:2002 will be greater than with past versions of automotive standards. In fact, a key phase for the internal auditor is: plan, plan, plan. The internal auditor is now responsible for collecting/developing flowcharts, reviewing customer data, being able to understand and interpret statistical information about the current process, reviewing previous audits of the target area, using questions from managers that might relate to the target area, and

preparing a customer focus checklist that is specific to that area related to the available information. To accomplish all of this, the internal
auditor will need time to prepare before going
into an area to conduct an audit.

COLLECT/DEVELOP FLOWCHARTS

The basic components of any process are the following: there is a process owner(s), the process is
defined, the process is documented as needed, the
linkages of the process are established, and the
process is being monitored. With these facts in
place, there should already be a process flowchart
available for any given process in the organization that an internal auditor might be responsible to audit. However, if the internal auditor is
unable to find something in written form, then
they (the auditor) must create one for that target
area. This is required to be able to see how the
process is working toward satisfying customers
and to identify the linkages that might be or
have the potential of causing any issues.

Flowcharts can be done in any variety of ways,
which goes beyond the scope of this book (see
Memory Jogger II or any other reference that
contains flowchart construction techniques); however, one primary factor should be consistency
within the organization. Thus, everyone should

be following the basic same format in creating flowcharts within the company.

IDENTIFY CUSTOMER INFORMATION

Using the flowchart, the internal auditor should be able to identify who the customers are (both internal and external) for each process that is to be audited. "Customer" can be identified as the next step in the operation(s); the next person who will touch the product, service, or information; the next department that will work on the product; the next plant that will receive the product; or the person who will ultimately use the product that they purchase.

For any given process, there may be various customers who may need to be consulted as to the usefulness of the product, service, or information. For many plants, the next operation in making a product should be considered as the primary customer and thus, information about how good the part worked in the customer's process should be examined by the internal auditor. Each operation/process is required to know how well their products, services, or information work for their customers.

The next step then is to find out, prior to the audit, what data are being tracked to demonstrate customer satisfaction. If internal customer data are being monitored, then are they in the form of control charts, run charts, bar charts, or other means? Do the data indicate a stable or improving process? (Remember that stability is different from improvement.) If external customer data are being monitored, in what format are they being collected and how useful are the data? Is it possible that missing information could cause the organization problems in the future? If so, then a PAR needs to be written to address the missing information.

DEVELOP AN AUDIT STRATEGY

The *audit matrix* (see Figure 5.1) shows the relationships between the different types of audits. The internal auditor will be mostly concerned with the internal audit slice of the matrix. Thus, are you being instructed to conduct a product, process, system, management, or compliance audit? Will the audit be conducted in a functional, departmental, or desk format? With these decisions in place, you will be able to plan a strategy of how to approach the audit and how to set up your checklist.

Some hints:

* *Product audit.* You can start at the beginning, the end, or anywhere in

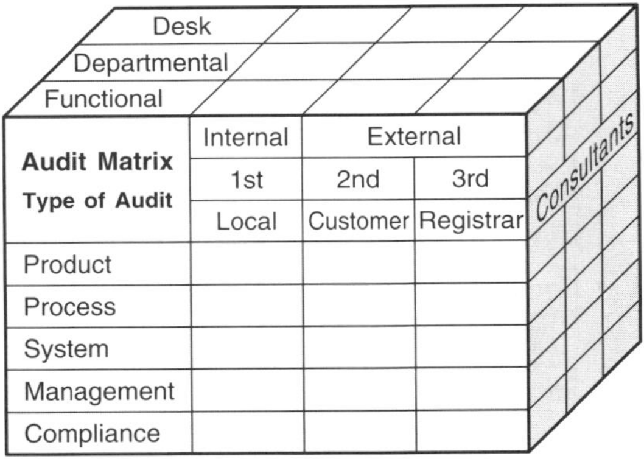

Figure 5.1   Audit matrix.

between. Look for sequential paths where the product is being made and what could possibly go wrong during production.

- *Process audit.* Is the process accurately flowcharted? Look for the linkage between the boxes on the flowchart to ensure smooth transitions of parts and information.

- *System audit.* Look at the entire process to ensure that things are running as intended, similar to the process audit but on a larger scale that covers more of the entire organization.

- *Management audit.* Since top management has a much bigger picture about what is happening in an organization, they may direct certain things to be reviewed within the company. These are usually specific items or areas that need reviewing and can be selected at any time.

- *Compliance audit.* Usually associated with the environmental standards now and is used to ensure that procedures and policies are being followed as written. It is expected in this type of auditing that things have one right way of being done and that people are in fact following the exact method.

CUSTOMIZE YOUR AUDIT CUSTOMER FOCUS CHECKLIST

Once the internal auditor has collected the information described previously, then an individualized customer focus checklist can be developed for the upcoming audit. It is not wise to just be given a predeveloped checklist the day of or the day before and try to audit an area with little or no preparation. One of the key outcomes of the internal audit under ISO/TS 16949:2002 is that the internal auditors should be writing more PARs

than CARs! To do this well, each of the aforementioned steps should be taken to familiarize
yourself with the area that you are about to
audit. Thus, creating a customized checklist on
what you have reviewed will lead to a much
better plan of audit.

THE TURTLE MODEL

The turtle diagram is becoming a common check-
sheet method of data collection used by internal
auditors concerning the process being investigated.
This is one method of ensuring the information is
collected and that the overall process is reviewed
for possible areas for improvement. It has been
found that once data are put on a page in a format like this, people get a better understanding
of the process. (Ever heard that a picture is worth
a thousand words?) Thus, the turtle diagram
becomes one of the primary reports that auditors
can turn in with their audit findings.

SUMMARY

The internal auditor has a lot more planning to
do than in past audits. Table 5.1 gives an
overview of what needs to be accomplished prior
to actually going onto the shop floor. Using this

as a checklist will assist the internal auditor to ensure that everything is being covered.

Table 5.1   Automotive internal auditor planning matrix.

1	Audit intent	What is the intent for this audit? Product, process, system, management, or compliance by function, department, or desk (see audit matrix).
2	Audit team	Who will be involved in auditing this area(s)?
3	Flowchart	Process map, value stream analysis, or other related documents.
4	Customer data	Both internal and external—may include survey information, e-mails, trip reports, information logs, or other records that the area(s) keep to stay informed about what customer satisfaction.
5	Current process data	Histograms, run charts, control charts, Pareto diagrams, bar charts, and so on, relating to an understanding of how the process is behaving.
6	Results of previous audits	What has been said in the past for this area(s). Are there any open CARs or PARs?

continued

continued

7	Area concerns matrix	During the top management review meetings, has anything been commented on for this area(s) that needs to be investigated further?
8	Questions from training manager	The training manager is responsible for training effectiveness and should provide questions of training programs that certain individuals from the target area(s) need to answer. (See Rice and Munro, "Training Evaluation Model," in *The Certified Quality Engineer Handbook*, Benbow, Berger, Elshennawy, and Walker [Milwaukee: ASQ Quality Press, 2002]: 37–38.)
9	Checklist	Each audit should have a tailored checklist of items for this particular area(s) for this particular audit.

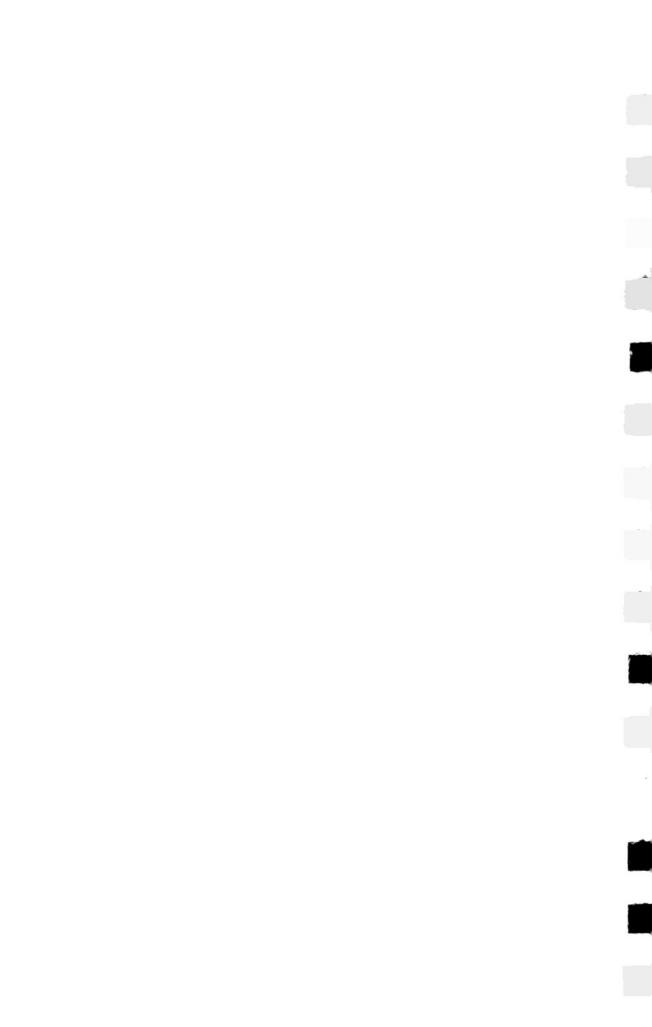

6

Conducting the Audit

The process of conducting audits will basically remain the same for many automotive plants and goes beyond the scope of this handbook. The reference section lists several books if a review of internal auditing procedures is desired. This chapter will look at several key items to be reviewed while conducting the automotive internal audit that go beyond basic ISO 9001 internal auditing.

QUESTIONS (MATRIX)

As has been stated, there is a new audit focus (customer satisfaction) in ISO/TS 16949:2002. Internal auditors will need to develop a new set of questions with the initial intent of, "How is the customer being satisfied?" and "How do we know?" Table 6.1 lists some additional items to think about while conducting the audit. It covers

Table 6.1   Data collection (audit findings) and analysis.

Questions for consideration	What are the results of the process? Is the process focused on the customer? What problems are really being addressed? What are the goals? What is going on in the operation? Where is the audit leading? What questions are you going to ask and of whom? What do you need to collect and can you stay within the audit time?
Auditing activities	Conduct open meeting or area introduction Confirm with auditee the process to be audited, who will be involved, and how the information will be shared Validate the process flow Start the audit trail using the prepared checklist for this audit Collect, organize, and analyze audit findings Complete appropriate paperwork
Organization considerations	Identify the level of support from leadership. How might this impact the quality of the process? Be prepared to respond to defensiveness and denial concerning the data, results, and conclusions drawn.

continued

continued

Pitfalls to avoid	Not understanding the situation to know what is really happening in the process.
	Nitpicking
	Not providing feedback to those who provided information
	Inappropriate analysis of incorrect assumptions
	Allowing audit trail to take you too far from audit scope
	Not having an SME available when needed
Potential tools	Interviewing skills
	Listening skills
	Basic auditing techniques
	Checksheets

questions for consideration, auditing activities, organization considerations, pitfalls to avoid, and potential tools. The internal auditors will be using their uniquely developed checklists and flowcharts during the audit and possibly the turtle diagram (or variation thereof) to collect data on the process being audited.

IATF FOCUS CLAUSES

The following list (Table 6.2) has been identified by the IATF and used in formal sanctioned training as being high-focus clauses of ISO/TS

Table 6.2   ISO/TS 16949:2002 structure.

4.2.2	Quality manual
5.1.1	Process efficiency
5.4.1.1	Quality objectives—supplemental
5.6.1.1	Quality management system performance
6.2.2.2	Training
6.2.2.4	Employee motivation and empowerment
6.3.1	Plant, facility, and equipment planning
6.3.2	Contingency plans
7.1	Planning of product realization
7.1.4	Change control
7.2.1.1	Customer-designated special characteristics
7.3	Design and development
7.3.1.1	Multidisciplinary approach
7.3.2.3	Special characteristics
7.3.6.3	Product approval process
7.4.1	Purchasing process
7.4.1.2	Supplier quality management system development
7.4.3.2	Supplier monitoring
7.5.1.4	Preventive and predictive maintenance
7.5.1.5	Management of production tooling
7.5.1.7	Feedback of information from service
7.5.1.8	Service agreement with customer
7.5.4.1	Customer-owned production tooling
7.6.3	Laboratory requirements
8.1.2	Knowledge of basic statistical concepts
8.2.1.1	Customer satisfaction—supplemental
8.2.2.2	Manufacturing process audit

continued

continued

8.2.3.1	Monitoring and measurement of manufacturing processes
8.3.4	Customer waiver
8.4.1	Analysis and use of data
8.5.1.2	Manufacturing process improvement
8.5.2.3	Corrective-action impact
8.5.3	Preventive action

16949:2002. This means that registrars are supposed to pay particular attention to these items while conducting the registration audit. Top management and internal auditors will need to verify that these areas have been covered according to the top management planning process for the organization.

DATA ANALYSIS

While analyzing an area, function, or department, the internal auditor needs to be observant of any number of things that are happening or could happen! He or she must keep an open mind to various possibilities, looking for ways to improve or optimize (the word the Japanese prefer) the operation. The internal auditor should be asking questions of operators such as: Who is the customer of this process and how do you know that you are meeting (exceeding) customer wants and needs? Do shop floor personnel know how and where the parts they make are being used? Internal auditors need to also be on the lookout for more than one flowchart or process map in the area (maintenance, production, safety, and so on) to see if these diagrams can be combined into one per area.

Statistical data analysis is something to be careful with. The main point here is to KISS (keep it simple statistician)! Are the data being collected in this area important? Is there too much data collection? Have the measurements for the processes been identified and is the data correlated to the process? Have linkages between the processes and the measurements been identified and correlated? The starting point for statistical data analysis should be the automotive core tools manuals. These books (APQP, FMEA, SPC, and MSA) were primarily designed as reference manuals (with the exception of PPAP) and can serve as a good foundation in how to collect and analyze data. Your organization should have at least one person who is very knowledgeable about data collection and analysis (possibly a statistician), and you as the internal auditor may need to ask that person for help in looking over data you find during the audit.

The use and understanding of data is a very important part of top management responsibility; however, many business schools in the United

States have traditionally done a poor job of training people in statistical tools. Thus, the internal auditor should be asking how managers, internal auditors, and others have been trained to analyze data and what additional training or application experience may be needed. Just creating bar or pie charts from a computer software package does not constitute data analysis!

SUMMARY

The internal auditor has a lot of things to remember while conducting a process audit! The use of process maps, customer focus checksheets, and the turtle diagram data collection tools should help the internal auditor stay focused on the task at hand of looking for ways to continually improve customer satisfaction.

7

Automotive Standard ISO/TS 16949:2002

The following section utilizes the outline of ISO/TS 16949:2002 and addresses some basic items that automotive internal auditors need to understand when conducting a process audit in an automotive plant. A code has been established here to help the internal auditor identify the relating documents that could impact the plant's ability to demonstrate effectiveness and continual improvement per requirements found in the standard.

Internal auditors are encouraged to make specific applications to their plant setting and to go beyond the items listed here to help ensure that the plant is meeting and exceeding customer requirements to enhance customer satisfaction. The issues/questions raised here are meant to be starters when addressing each clause during internal process audits.

Key Code

*	IATF focus item
(G)	More detail found in the IATF Guidance document
(R)	More detail found in the IATF Rules document
(DCX)	DaimlerChrysler Customer-Specific Requirements
(Ford)	Ford Motor Company Customer-Specific Requirements
(GM)	General Motors Corporation Customer-Specific Requirements
(APQP)	Core tool reference
(PPAP)	Core tool reference
(FMEA)	Core tool reference
(SPC)	Core tool reference
(MSA)	Core tool reference

Remember that the starting point in any review should be to look at the following four items:

1. Customer data

2. Process output data

3. Actual operations

4. What the policy and procedures state

Then ask the question: *Does what we see and hear* make sense *in enhancing customer satisfaction?* If there is even a slight question in your mind, then consider writing a PAR on this process or operation in order to allow top management an opportunity to review this area during their next management review cycle. Your intuition contains a lot of intelligence. Do not make the mistake of ignoring it!

Please note that if you, as an internal auditor, have an opportunity to shadow or guide an external auditor, that person may not ask all of these questions. However, you should see the thread of thinking, given any particular element that they touch, during their audit of your organization. You as the internal auditor have a responsibility to ensure that your organization is using the standards to help improve customer satisfaction in everything that it does.

4.0 QUALITY MANAGEMENT SYSTEM

4.1 General requirements

Q *How does your plant plan to demonstrate continual improvement (versus continual change) of the QMS?*

If the quality manual is a doorstop or dust collector, then how effective can it be? You need to ensure that appropriate personnel (at a minimum, top management) know what is in the quality manual and are in fact using it on a regular basis to help run the plant to satisfy customer needs.

Q *Is the quality manual set up according to the new numbering system or is a conversion matrix being used?*

Q *What evidence of effective implementation is available? How has the company addressed letters "a" through "f" in section 4.1?*

4.1.1 General requirements—Supplemental

Q *Do problems arise with your suppliers that reach your customers?*

Even if the customer directs which supplier you must use, your plant is still responsible for the quality of your products/services to the customer.

Q *What continual improvement projects are available for review?*

Note that these are not the corrective-action items that have been taken, but preventive items. Top management *must* be able to distinguish between corrective actions and preventive actions.

4.2 Documentation requirements

4.2.1 General

Many plants still have a documented system as a result of QS-9000, which required that everything be documented. ISO 9001:2000 only "requires" six areas to have documented procedures (4.2.3, 4.2.4, 8.2.2, 8.3, 8.5.2, and 8.5.3) and ISO/TS 16949:2002 requires one additional documented procedure for 6.2.2.2. The plant's top management has the option to document any additional areas that they feel are necessary to enhance customer satisfaction. One primary question that the internal auditor needs to ask with regard to all documented procedures or work instructions is:

Q *Is this document used on a regular basis? If the answer is no, then why is this procedure documented?*

The automotive internal auditor needs to be willing to ask the tough questions about:

- Why processes are documented.

- Whether some of these should be part of training programs or listed in other formats that will ensure that work is completed in a means to enhance customer satisfaction.

The top management *must* be able to answer the question about the adequacy of procedures in context of the complexity of the organization.

While conducting the internal audit, auditors should ask personnel:

- How the quality policy and QMS effects/ affects the work that each person is performing.

- How does the current QMS show effective planning, operation, and control of plant processes?

4.2.2 Quality manual * (Ford)

All automotive plants have a quality manual, but is it a document that is used to help run the plant or something that only the quality manager knows how to use? The new portion of the standard states that a description of the interaction between the processes discussed in the QMS is present. Top management is responsible for knowing and controlling these interactions in an effort to enhance customer satisfaction.

Note: This clause is a high-focus area identified by the IATF. Ford requires that the entire plant be covered by the registration audit, thus the internal auditors should ensure that all aspects of the plant are in fact inspected during the yearly review cycle.

4.2.3 Control of documents (Ford)

The automotive industry has long required control of documents used in the production process of parts/services to customers. This clause continues this requirement and top management (more than just the management representative) must ensure that the plant is proactive in ensuring that the most current documents are in fact used at the point of production. Thus, look for a control master list or other means of ensuring that top management is involved with the overall system. Have letters "a" through "g" been handled in an effective manner for this organization?

Q *What evidence can top management show to demonstrate that the documentation process leads to satisfied customers?*

This is one of the clauses requiring a documented procedure.

Q *How does this process contribute to customer satisfaction?*

Note that Ford requires an annual review of all quality system documents (policies, procedures, and work instructions, and so on).

4.2.3.1 Engineering specifications (Ford)

Q *What evidence exists to demonstrate that this clause is being met, especially the two-week requirement?*

Q *Has the organization ever received a complaint against their engineering change process and is the corrective action still appropriate?*

Q *If no complaint has been issued against this organization in the past, what preventive action has top management put in place to prevent any issues from arising?*

4.2.4 Control of records (Ford)

Q *Is the records retention system effective in storing, maintaining, and retrieving what is supposed to be kept, and are things being disposed of as indicated?*

This is one of the clauses requiring a documented procedure.

Q *How does this process contribute to customer satisfaction?*

4.2.4.1 Record retention (DCX-GM)

Internal auditors need to know something about the regulatory requirements relating to records and record retention to ensure that the organization is in regulatory compliance.

Q *How does the organization manage customer requirement information, and where can it be found?*

5.0 MANAGEMENT RESPONSIBILITY

5.1 Management commitment (Ford)

The responsibility is on top management (this is the top person at your manufacturing site and his or her immediate direct reports—including finance and human resources) to provide evidence that they are truly committed to satisfying and enhancing customer satisfaction! Actions and records of actions taken must back up words.

Q *What evidence can be shown that top management has used employee feedback and preventive actions have been taken to ensure that products and services have been of the highest quality level?*

Q *What has been done to address letters "a"
through "e"?*

5.1.1 Process efficiency (Ford) *

Top management can delegate the responsibility to get work done, however, the accountability for the QMS is still ultimately held by the top management!

Q *Thus, how is top management reviewing and
supporting the overall organization to ensure
that product realization satisfies and exceeds
customer requirements?*

Look through past management meeting records to see if things like corrective and especially preventive action items have been addressed.

Q *Have internal audit reports (corrective actions
and preventive actions) been addressed?*

Q *What evidence exists that top management
is using past survey results to manage the
business?*

Q *Do the employee surveys align with what you
are hearing on the plant floor?*

5.2 Customer focus (Ford)

QS-9000 and ISO/TS 16949:1999 based their focus on the organization's processes. Now the focus of the entire organization is supposed to be the customer and customer satisfaction! This should also include the internal customers.

Q *How has the organization made this switch in basic philosophy?*

This should go far beyond the quality department's ongoing monitoring of the process and dealing with customer complaints.

Q *What is top management doing to ensure that the entire organization is focusing on all customers?*

5.3 Quality policy (partial new)

Every automotive company has a quality policy.

Q *What are the measurable goals in meeting that policy and how do people in the company apply the policy to their particular jobs?*

There needs to be linkage between the business plan, the quality policy, the QMS, and the day-to-day operations of the plant.

Q *Are each of the letters "a" through "e" addressed?*

Q *What evidence is available that the top management is truly looking for opportunities to continually improve the overall process?*

5.4 Planning

5.4.1 Quality objectives (Ford)

Many automotive plants are moving toward displaying some form of measurement boards (score board, balanced scorecards, and so on) at the end of production lines and even in office areas. This should be the starting point for many audit activities, as these measures should directly link to customer satisfaction. The acronym SQDCME stands for safety, quality, delivery, cost, morale, and environment. If there are no such measures available, then some serious observations need to be made.

Q *How is top management focusing on the customer, and how do they encourage everyone in the product realization process to improve their processes?*

If you have no measure, then how do you know where you are? This should all be linked back to the business plan for the plant.

5.4.1.1 Quality objectives—supplemental *

The overall measurement system for the plant needs to have ties to measures that relate to everyone in the organization culminating with a top level set of measures for the top management. One of the indicators (5.6.1.1) must be cost of poor quality calculations and relate to the business plan.

Q *Has this information (measureables from around the plant) been discussed at the management level meetings?*

5.4.2 Quality management system planning (Ford)

One of the primary tools that top management should use to review the overall plant system is the internal quality audits of the plant's QMS.

Q *Is there evidence that audits are being conducted to the process approach and that top management is taking preventive actions based on PARs and other information (such as the employee suggestion program) provided during reviews of the system?*

5.5 Responsibility, Authority and Communication

5.5.1 Responsibility and authority

Q *Are the appropriate people in the plant given the responsibility and authority to do the jobs they are tasked with?*

This may sound strange, but many organizations dump anything that has the word "quality" onto the quality department! If this is done, (for example, with APQP, which is an engineering function) then the intent of the standard is *not* being followed and top management has not truly established an accountability process within the plant!

5.5.1.1 Responsibility for quality

There are four items called out here—each needs to be validated by the internal auditors.

Q *Can you demonstrate that if something has gone wrong, the appropriate people (not just the quality department) have responded to root-cause analysis?*

Q *How are PARs being used?*

Q *Do the operators on the line really have the authority to stop production? Or does it only look that way?*

Q *Are there people on all shifts who actually monitor product quality?*

5.5.2 Management representative

Unfortunately, this person is usually the top quality person in the plant! In the old standards (QS and TS 1999), this person was called on to ensure that everything in the QMS was done; now it is only to ensure that the documentation system is in place. Top management must ensure that every department in the organization (design, sales, manufacturing, delivery, and so on) is involved and committed to meeting and enhancing customer satisfaction.

5.5.2.1 Customer representative (Ford)

Again, this does not have to be the quality department's responsibility, but top management must ensure that the needs/wants of customers are identified in all aspects of the plant's planning and operations. Someone *must* represent the customer's point of view in any activity that might impact customer satisfaction (that is, APQP, PPAP, MSA, CARs, PARs, and so on).

5.5.3 Internal communication (new)

This is a new clause in the standard, and internal auditors will need to review the communication channels and timeliness of responses in the plant.

Q *How quickly does information flow and what records are kept to indicate timely and effective communications?*

Q *What plans are in place to continually improve the internal communication within the plant?*

5.6 Management review (Ford)

5.6.1 General

Q *Who does top management identify to be their customers, both internal and external, and how are reviews conducted to ensure that the needs of both groups are being met?*

This question is very involved and there is no one right answer. Many managers will have to be challenged (professionally, of course) to really think about this, especially as it relates to the employees of the organization. Internal auditors will sometimes hear very different things from top management and from employees about what is going on around the plant. This is an indication that top management is *not* "tuned in" to what is happening on the floor or in the office and thus need to be challenged in this category! If the internal auditor has any questions about how to challenge top management here, you should seek advice from your supervisor or, if she or he is the person you need to challenge, some other manager whom you feel that you can talk with in confidence. Also, it is best in difficult situations to have the audit team report the results instead of an individual. This delivery method usually helps get across messages that may be difficult for managers to hear.

5.6.1 Quality management system performance *

Q *What is the top management reviewing and how often are things evaluated?*

Two common acronyms are SQDCME (safety, quality, delivery, cost, morale, and environment) and QCD+E (quality, cost, delivery, plus environment). The measurement process should be available to everyone who affects the quality of the products leaving the organization (which means everyone). Thus, the internal auditor must look at how managers are ensuring coverage of this requirement through the review of data. We will look at the type of measurements in category 8.

5.6.2 Review input (new) (Ford)

This section gives specific items that managers must be able to demonstrate have been reviewed during their "periodic meetings." Some of these should already be in the old system, but new items can include: 1) results of internal and external audits, 2) status of preventive actions (corrective actions are usually done), 3) follow-up actions from previous top management reviews, and 4) recommendations for improvement.

Q *Do the minutes of meetings indicate complete coverage of all the items listed in this section?*

5.6.2.1 Review input—Supplemental

The top management can usually talk a very good game here.

Q *Is there evidence that they have actually done an analysis of potential failure of the system and taken action to prevent such failures?*

The simplest proof would be a quality management system failure mode and effects analysis (QMS-FMEA). Few managers have actually done this.

Q *Can the internal auditor find documented evidence that the risk management process of an FMEA concept has actually been done?*

5.6.3 Review output (new)

Q *Is it evident from the minutes of the management meetings that the managers made decisions based on the three items listed in the standard?*

Q *What improvement or resources were discussed?*

Q *Is there evidence that this has been or is being carried out in daily activities?*

6.0 RESOURCE MANAGEMENT

6.1 Provision of resources

A challenge in this element will be the balance between lean manufacturing and the ability to get the work done in a way that satisfies customers. Internal auditors should not be afraid to raise issues here as preventive action items as a cautionary element for top management review! One real challenge for many organizations will be to have the staff needed to get the current work done.

Q *Are there enough time and resources to work on continual improvement activities?*

6.2 Human resources

6.2.1 General

Q *Are people who are doing assigned tasks in the organization competent to do that work?*

This question needs to be raised for all personnel in the plant from the sweeper to the very top manager! There is no one right way to ensure competency for a given job; however, due to the continual improvement of work to be done, everyone needs to have an ongoing training program. Thus, the auditor should be asking:

Q *What training have you had in the last year (or whatever the reporting period is) and how are you using what you learned to help improve customer satisfaction?*

The training manager may ask the internal auditor to ask certain personnel questions relating to training and then to give a summary of

these responses back to the training manager.
This is part of the Rice and Munro Training Evaluation Model (ASQ CQE Handbook) that can be used to evaluate the current training program for the organization.

6.2.2 Competence, awareness and training (Ford)

There is a lot in this section with the five items that are asked!

1. Your organization must have job descriptions for each job title in your organization.

    Q *Are these job descriptions completed and do they list the competencies for each job (this includes each of the top managers' roles)?*

    Note: For the lab job description, a general listing will not meet the requirements for ISO/TS 16949:2002 clause 7.6.3.1 Internal laboratory, which asks for specific competency requirements for laboratory personnel.

2. What is your organization using besides formal training programs to help people learn and grow?
    Formal training should be only one piece of the top management plan for learning within the organization.

Q *How is top management using other learning interventions and is it in a planned manner (that is, plant and staff meetings, on-the-job training, books, audio tapes, job aids/banners, one-on-one coaching, and so on)?*

3. The use of surveys at the end of formal training courses is usually the weakest form of training evaluation.

Q *What is your organization doing to truly learn how effective all of its learning interventions are?*

See references for ASTD, ISPI, and Benbow, Berger, Elshennawy, and Walker (2002), chapter 2, "Quality Management Training."

4. Do people performing various work assignments understand how what they do fits into customer satisfaction (internal and external)?

One area to check for understanding is to look at the FMEAs and see if people recognize anything for which the customer or your own organization has given some form of special classification.

Q *How are special or significant characteristics being handled and dealt with?*

5. This is the same as the old QS-9000 in that records are to be kept on everyone's training program.

   Q *Are records complete with the non-traditional training items (that is, all-hands meetings, special discussions, books, audio tapes, and so on)?*

   Q *Are the training records being kept separate from other personal information such as medical histories and personnel information?*

   Note: In the United States, it is a federal law that three sets of information need to be kept on each employee (personnel, medical, and training). You as an internal auditor can *only* view the training records. If everything is in one folder, then a human resources person must be able to pull out *only* the training records for your review.

6.2.2.1 Product design skills (Ford)

(See the IATF Guidance to ISO/TS 16949:2002 clause 6.2.2.1 for a starter list of tools that your organization should be using.)

Q *How are design techniques identified by your organizations?*

This is required even if you are not design-responsible, as your organization must be prepared to discuss work with those who are design-responsible! Also, within your organization, internal special characteristics must be identified for statistical observation. This element goes beyond formal training.

Q *What else has top management done to ensure that engineers are prepared for this role (that is, customer visits, conference attendance, books, audio tapes, videos, and so on)?*

6.2.2.2 Training * (Ford)

This is one of the clauses requiring a documented procedure. There is an entire profession built around the field of adult learning. The formal term for this particular activity is called a *training needs assessment* (TNA).

Q *What is your organization doing toward continual improvement in the professional training arena that should lead to the identification of what people need to know for particular job assignments based on what has been identified for each activity in 6.2.2 a?*

See references for ASTD and ISPI.

Q *How does this process contribute to customer satisfaction?*

6.2.2.3 Training on the job (Ford)

Q *Is the training that people are receiving on the job being recorded in some format?*

Q *Are the people doing the work (plant or staff) aware of the consequences of doing their particular job assignment in a poor or unacceptable manner?*

Q *Does each person know how his or her work affects the customers (both internal and external)?*

6.2.2.4 Employee motivation and empowerment * (Ford)

This is one of the more difficult and subjective items in the standard! Many managers believe that they are doing a really good job in this category. However, the internal auditor should be looking for evidence that people are motivated to do good work all of the time. Compare the number of CARs to PARs in the organization (there should be many more PARs). Then look at the number of customer complaints (there should be a number of measures for this). If the internal and external parts per million (ppm) is above acceptable customer limits, then suggestions are not coming in quick enough from employees, or management is not responding to workers! Something is not right!

6.3 Infrastructure

Q *What can be found to demonstrate that top management has determined and is continuing to review the structural needs of the organization?*

Q *Does there seem to be enough room for everything that needs to get done?*

Q *Are safety items (that is, mirrors at corners, 5S, and so on) being addressed within the organization?*

6.3.1 Plant, facility, and equipment planning * (Ford)

Q *What evidence is available that a cross-functional team actually developed and continues to review the needs of your organization?*

Note: Though several names may be present, these people may or may not have actually met on this topic.

Q *Also, do the minutes or other evidence indicate which person took the role of the customer representative in these meetings?*

6.3.2 Contingency plans * (Ford)

Q *Beyond what QS-9000 required, are there plans now for key equipment failure and field returns?*

Field returns can include a customer calling to tell your organization that product shipment has been rejected and you need to send immediate replacement parts that do not contain the same nonconformance!

6.4 Work environment

Q *How has top management determined the overall work setting that will be used to meet customer requirements?*

Q *Are there customer complaints that indicate that your organization is not prepared to meet the overall need of the external customers?*

Q *What is top management doing to ensure that internal customer needs are being met?*

6.4.1 Personnel safety to achieve product quality (new)

OSHA has recently changed the requirements for reporting incidents in a plant environment!

Q *What is top management doing to ensure that both product and employee safety is maintained at all times?*

6.4.2 Cleanliness of premises (Ford)

This may sound like a subjective question, but to quote an old Japanese saying: "If top management cannot give employees clean restrooms, how can they get anything else done correctly?"

Q *Is there trash lying around the plant?*

Q *Is an effective 5S program or other method in place to ensure that things are where they need to be?*

Q *Are sweepings picked up in a timely manner?*

7.0 PRODUCT REALIZATION

Note: If your plant does not have design responsibility, only element portions of 7.3, dealing with aspects of the product design, may be excluded from the internal audit.

7.1 Planning of product realization * (Ford)

Q *Has your organization taken into account aspects of the APQP manual and any other related processes or procedures that your plant may be required to accomplish in the advanced quality planning process?*

Q *Is top management actively planning the quality of products and services for customers? This should include all aspects of the organization and cover all personnel.*

Q *What are the specific activities that your organization does during APQP?*

Q *Have there been issues with past launches and if so what has been done to prevent the same issue in the future?*

Q *What is top management doing in advanced quality planning (resources, timing, training, travel, and so on) to be proactive and prevent issues from arising with customers?*

As with the entire standard, the questioning should start with customer satisfaction.

Q *Thus, in this case, are customers happy with how the organization is doing in the planning process?*

Q *What are the customer measurables being used?*

Many organizations have not traditionally measured this aspect of their organization, but are now required to. Please remember that the APQP manual includes the planning for production and feedback on the overall system.

Q *Is everything in your operation running smoothly for both external and internal customers?*

Q *If not, then what was missed in the advanced quality planning process that needs to be changed for the next product cycle?*

The APQP is supposed to be the planning of everything that will be done during production and even how parts and information will be handled post production, until tooling scrap authorization is received from the customer!

7.1.1 Planning of product realization

Q *How has the APQP team at your organization accounted for any customer-specific requirements or other appropriate needs of the customer?*

Q *How does your organization keep track of international, national, or local governmental regulations that might impact future products?*

Q *What are APQP team members doing, or being allowed to do, to ensure continual improvement (training, conference, customer meetings, and so on)?*

7.1.2 Acceptance criteria (Ford)

Q *Does your organization hold to zero defects (especially for attribute items)?*

Q *What does your customer information say?*

Q *If your plant is shipping any nonconforming product, then what is being done either in a corrective manner or preventive manner to get to zero defects?*

Q *Are the plans working?*

7.1.3 Confidentiality

Q *Is all information relating to parts under development being safeguarded?*

Q *One area many organizations miss: What access do visitors have to your information?*

There should be a sign in/sign out process for all visitors (this is also for safety reasons), and if they come in contact with new products under development, then a confidentiality statement should be signed by those individuals. This could go so far as to check contract housekeeping people who might be cleaning offices where engineers have prototypes, drawings, and so on, sitting on their desks at night.

7.1.4 Change control * (DCX-GM)

One standard joke is: "Do customers ever change their minds?" It is a well-known fact that many organizations are constantly having to change things during the design and development phases of APQP and sometimes even into full production. This constant changing, sometimes to hard tools, causes many issues for suppliers. The questions should be:

Q *What is your organization doing to plan for the inevitable changes that will occur during the APQP process?*

Q *What preventive steps are the APQP team taking to ensure that changes are being kept to a minimum? Once major expenses have been made what steps have been taken to prevent future changes?*

For this to be done well, top management must put a lot more commitment into the up-front planning phases than traditionally have been done in the past.

Q *What is top management doing and what is their role in the APQP process?*

This is not just a delegation issue—top management must be involved to make this work to improve customer satisfaction!

7.2 Customer-related processes

7.2.1 Determination of requirements related to the product (Ford)

The items called out in "a" through "d" have to be planned for (note the APQP team involvement) prior to the actual need for the issue.

Q *How is the organization planning and what are the outcomes of past planning?*

Here we may have to look at the government as a customer as well! The internal auditor should be looking for trends in satisfaction to things such as OSHA-reportable accidents (note that in January 2003 the reporting criteria was changed by OSHA and thus the plant numbers might look worse than before) and other items that relate to this criterion. One question that might be asked is:

Q *How do you know that we are meeting all state, national, and international requirements?*

*7.2.1.1 Customer designated special characteristics * (DCX-Ford-GM-Guidance)*

Note the very high focus on this element!

Q *What records are available to demonstrate that your plant has met all requirements for designation, documentation, and control of special characteristics?*

Q *Does the information flow logically through all aspects of the paperwork: from the APQP minutes, the various FMEAs, the various control plans, and down to operator work instructions?*

7.2.2 Review of requirements related to the product

If your plant is part of a larger company, just saying that corporate assigned a product to your plant will no longer work! Every plant must have a formal acceptance process (that is documented with records) for all new product brought into the plant. Top management must take charge of this and be able to demonstrate to auditors (internal or external) how and why parts were allowed to enter the plant.

Q *In essence, the internal auditor should ask to see the needs assessment for each new product that comes into the plant.*

7.2.2.1 Review of requirements related to the product (Ford)

Where customers have approved deviation from the previous requirements, it must be in writing.

Q *What process does your organization have to maintain such records?*

7.2.2.2 Organization manufacturing feasibility (Ford-Guidance)

Q *Can your manufacturing unit actually make the part as designed?*

In trying to meet the customer wants, a number of complaints arise from poor designs. The design review and APQP team must address these issues prior to spending a lot of time in the process design phase of APQP.

Q *If you can't produce it, then why is your top management allowing time to be spent on it?*

7.2.3 Customer communication (GM) (new)

The internal auditor needs to look at all contact points of current communication with customers (shipping departments, production contacts, engineering contacts, management, delivery, and so on).

Q *How effectively are we communicating today?*

Q *Is the communication via electronic, fax, phone, visitations, or other means?*

Q *What is the overall customer satisfaction with our communication process?*

Q *What data do we have to show that we are working to continually improve communication with customers?*

7.2.3.1 Customer communication— supplemental (Ford-GM-G)

Q *Have we had any complaints concerning specific data interchanges with customers?*

Q *What is being done to prevent issues in the future?*

7.3 Design and development (possible exclusions) *

Author's note: Differences in requirements that internal auditors must be aware of in 7.3 for design responsible (black box) or non–design responsible (gray box) suppliers have been identified. If no distinction is made, then everyone must comply with that clause.

7.3.1 Design and development planning (Ford)

Black Box Supplier:

Q *How has top management established a preventive process to ensure that the design process works to effectively deliver customer satisfaction?*

Q *What is being measured to demonstrate that customer satisfaction is being continually improved?*

Q *What could be done better?*

Gray Box Supplier:
Even if your plant does not have design responsibility, your top management must still verify
that the communication with those who are
designing the product is being conducted effectively for customer satisfaction.

7.3.1.1 Multidisciplinary approach *
(Ford-Guidance)

Black Box Supplier:
Resources are an issue in many plants. Top management must ensure that appropriate resources
are available as needed.

Q *Are actual cross-functional teams working
on the items (special characteristics, FMEA,
and control plans) and working toward
continual improvement?*

Gray Box Supplier:
Same as previous! You need to verify that actual
cross-functional teams are working on special
characteristics, FMEAs, and control plans in your
organization.

7.3.2 Design and development inputs

Black Box Supplier:
How does the design process function to ensure that customer designs meet the needs and wants of the user (QFD)? What data are available to show that the design process truly meets the customer's expectations?

Gray Box Supplier:
Is a system in place to gather information on what the design requirements are or on how the products were designed?

7.3.2.1 Product design input (Guidance)

Black Box Supplier:
The internal auditor needs to look for evidence of the design inputs and how these were derived from the customer-stated needs.

Q *Were customers happy with the design output?*

Q *How many changes did the customer require during the design process and why?*

Q *Design changes usually indicate a problem with something.*

Q *Were any of the issues related to your organization?*

Gray Box Supplier:
Not applicable to gray box suppliers.

7.3.2.2 Manufacturing process design (Guidance)

Black Box Supplier:
The internal auditor needs to look for evidence of the design outputs being used to help design the manufacturing process.

Q *What types of issues have occurred in the past?*

Q *How is current manufacturing knowledge being used to plan for future production?*

Q *How are the various methodologies Six Sigma, kaizen, lean manufacturing, error-proofing, and others being used to develop the manufacturing practices of tomorrow?*

Q *Where are prevention practices being applied?*

Q *Are cross-functional teams being used to plan for future production?*

Gray Box Supplier:
Same issues as for the black box suppliers. Just saying that some other group is design responsible has little bearing on your organization's need to plan for manufacturing.

7.3.2.3 Special characteristics * (Ford-Guidance)

Black Box Supplier:

Q *Are special characteristics (both customer and internal) being identified early and does the information flow through all of the organizational documentation (drawings, FMEAs, PPAP, control plans, and so on)?*

A possible suggestion might be to number the characteristics on the prints and use that same number system on all other documents to help in tracking these characteristics throughout the process.

Gray Box Supplier:
Gray box suppliers will need to track special characteristics also. The internal auditor should look at how their organization identifies, tracks, and maintains control of these high-focus items.

7.3.3 Design and development outputs

Black Box Supplier:

Q *What available data show that the customers of the design process are satisfied with the design outputs?*

Q *Without customer satisfaction information, how can engineering know how well they are doing?*

Q *Many organizations try to make the engineering group the leading entity for new products, but will customers really appreciate the technology involved during use of the final product?*

Gray Box Supplier:
Internal auditors at gray box suppliers will not have to audit this element.

Q *Ask engineering how feedback is given to those who are design responsible.*

Q *How can communications be improved?*

Q *How can prevention be built into the design process to make things easier for your organization?*

7.3.3.1 Product design outputs—Supplemental (Guidance)

Black Box Supplier:

Q *Are the items listed in the standard available for customers?*

Q *Are the customers of the design engineering process satisfied with what is received?*

Q *How many changes have occurred in the past and are any being currently planned?*

Q *Was this due to poor planning in the first place?*

Q *What is being done with lessons learned to ensure that future engineers do not make the same mistakes or inadvertently cause the same issues in the future?*

Gray Box Supplier:
Gray box suppliers can exclude this part of the standard.

Q *However, are the items listed being received by the manufacturing engineering group and are they happy with what is received?*

7.3.3.2 Manufacturing process design output (Ford-Guidance)

Q *Are the items listed in the standard available for production personnel use?*

Q *Are people on the shop floor (internal customers) able to use the documents to produce products that meet customer requirements?*

Q *What is the satisfaction level of the shop floor with the manufacturing and other support functions?*

7.3.4 Design and development review (Ford)

Black Box Supplier:

Q *Is a plan in place and being used to ensure the design process is going to meet the customer needs?*

Q *How have changing customer wants and needs been addressed?*

Q *Have lessons learned from prior design and development processes been used?*

Q *How is information from the production floor impacting the design process?*

Q *Is a true cross-functional team (including shop floor people) involved with the review process?*

Gray Box Supplier:

Q *Have plant personnel been involved with the design-responsible groups prior to design release to the plant?*

Q *How is this documented?*

Q *How is information from the shop floor passed back to the design-responsible groups for use on future designs?*

7.3.4.1 Monitoring (Ford-Guidance)

Q *How is top management reviewing the design and development process?*

Q *Are measurements available and tracked relating to the customer effectiveness of the design process?*

7.3.5 Design and development verification (Ford)

Black Box Supplier:
According to APQP 2.3, design verification verifies that the product design meets the customer requirements derived from the activities described in "Plan and Define Program."

Q *What advance planning was established to verify the design of new products?*

Q *Do records indicate that designs were in fact verified, especially given any last-minute changes by the customer?*

Q *Were last-minute changes verified as to overall design for customer intent, manufacturability, assembly, and disassembly (environmental)?*

Gray Box Supplier:
Internal auditors at gray box suppliers should ask to see if the design outputs were used in creating the manufacturing process for the future parts.

7.3.6 Design and development validation (Guidance)

Black Box Supplier:
According to APQP 4.5, production validation testing refers to engineering tests that validate that products made from production tools and processes meet engineering standards.

Q *What advanced planning was established to validate that the products would work in manufacturing and assembly to create customer satisfaction with the end vehicle?*

Q *Are cross-functional teams involved?*

Q *Has top management been involved with various (note more than one) reviews during the overall design and development process?*

Q *How has customer satisfaction been measured (that is, PIST, PIPC, C_{pk}, P_{pk}, and so on)?*

Gray Box Supplier:
For internal auditors at gray box suppliers, review of how the plan was involved in the validation process may be critical to the plant successfully meeting all customer satisfaction requirements! This

may be especially true if your organization is in fact getting very little information from the design-responsible group/organization. Thus, you may need to be asking the same questions as the black box suppliers for this clause.

Q *How does the overall process of accepting new work at your plant validate that the part can actually be made to meet customer satisfaction?*

Q *How is top management reviewing new jobs coming into the plant to ensure that design intent and customer satisfaction is possible?*

7.3.6.1 Design and development validation— Supplement (DCX-Ford-GM-Guidance)

Q *Have all customer program requirements been identified as to how to meet the new program validation process? (That is, what is the planning for prototypes, full PPAP with all related information, and any other special items that may be required by the customer?)*

Q *How does your organization know what the requirements of the customer are?*

Q *Who at your organization is responsible for staying current with the customer requirements (especially any changing issues) and what is their training for this role?*

Q *Who at your organization fills the role of the customer representative for internal meetings?*

Q *How have they been trained for this and how are they staying current?*

7.3.6.2 Prototype program (Ford-Guidance)

Q *Is the entire PPAP process being followed by your organization? (If not, is there a written customer waiver?)*

Q *Is product at trial run actually being run-at-rate to simulate actual production conditions?*

Q *What metrics are being tracked to ensure customer satisfaction with the prototype process at your organization?*

Q *What preventive processes are in place to ensure customer satisfaction is realized?*

Q *Is top management involved in this overall process and is information on outcomes included in their review cycles?*

7.3.6.3 Product approval process * (Ford-Guidance)

Q *Has the customer's part submission warrant (PSW) been identified, completed, and filed according to the customer's requirements?*

Q *What metrics are being tracked to ensure customer satisfaction?*

Q *Are all aspects of PPAP being followed according to the customer wants (versus the simplest way for your organization)?*

7.3.7 Control of design and development changes (DCX-GM)

All changes (customer, supplier, or our own organization's) must be tracked, validated, and verified before being incorporated into production.

Q *How is this handled within your organization?*

Q *Is the system having positive results on customer satisfaction?*

Q *How does top management review such changes to ensure customer satisfaction?*

7.4 Purchasing

7.4.1 Purchasing process *

Q *How does the purchasing function evaluate, select, and monitor suppliers to ensure customer satisfaction?*

Q *Do all operating units in your organization (engineering, purchasing, production, and quality) agree on your supplier's value to achieving the end product?*

Q *Does purchasing have an advance quality planning process for suppliers to follow that ensures product conformance?*

Q *How does the purchasing record keeping on suppliers add value to the overall process?*

7.4.1.1 Regulatory conformity (Ford)

There is a growing need to ensure that everyone is following governmental regulatory requirements. Many organizations have added wording to the boilerplate of the purchase order to tell suppliers about this requirement.

Q *How does your purchasing group ensure regulatory conformance?*

7.4.1.2 Supplier quality management system development * (DCX-Ford-GM-Guidance)

Note the close attention paid to this clause by all components of the IAOB process! Supplier development is more than just asking that the supplier get registered to ISO 9001:2000.

Q *What is your organization doing to help develop your plant's suppliers?*

Q *Is the effort value-added and effective to overall customer satisfaction?*

Q *How does top management measure and know that the efforts are working?*

Q *How is compliance to ISO/TS 16949:2002 being planned for each supplier?*

7.4.1.3 Customer-approved sources (Ford)

Q *Do any of your customers require specified (approved) suppliers to be used by your plant?*

Q *Are these sources being used?*

If so, then everything in 7.4.1.2 applies to those required suppliers as well!

7.4.2 Purchasing information

Q *Does your organization ensure that suppliers are given all information needed to ensure your customer satisfaction?*

Q *Are there any current supplier problems?*

Q *How are these problems (if any) affecting your customers?*

Q *What is being done to prevent reoccurrence?*

7.4.3 Verification of purchased product

Suppliers are responsible for verifying production capabilities and products prior to shipping parts to your plant.

Q *How is this being accomplished and who is monitoring the efforts?*

Q *How does your plant know that it is getting what has been requested of the supplier?*

7.4.3.1 Incoming product quality (Ford)

Q *Is one or more of the five techniques listed in the standard actually used in your plant?*

Q *Have there been problems?*

Q *How is the overall system moving to prevent problems from occurring in the first place?*

7.4.3.2 Supplier monitoring * (Ford-Guidance)

Q *Is appropriate statistical analysis (typically run or trend charts) being used for each of the four items listed in the standard to monitor the supplier's performance?*

Q *Is supplier monitoring changed in accordance with the monitoring methods?*

7.5 Production and service provision (Ford)

7.5.1 Control of production and service provision

The internal auditor needs to think about the six items listed in the standard plus the eight sub-clauses (7.5.1.1 through 7.5.1.8) and linkages between (see the chapter on process auditing) activities/items. Again, the starting point for a lot of process auditing is to look at customer feedback and the trends of customer satisfaction! Based on what has gone wrong with your system in the past, ask:

Q *Where may the problems be coming from in the plans?"*

Q *Do the scheduling, production, and preventive maintenance people have a schedule that looks at upcoming work a month in the future (most plants only plan out a day or two)?*

Q *Is there a consistent information flow from engineering to production workers, from customer schedules to shop floor supervisors, from what is actually happening on the floor to top management reviews?*

Q *Is information available to the shop floor accurate and up to date?*

Q *Are the training, communication, and competence factors effective?*

Q *Are resources where and when they are needed?*

7.5.1.1 Control plan

Q *Can the internal auditor see linkage between the prototype control plans, prelaunch control plans, and the production control plans?*

Q *Can linkages be seen on the production control plan back to the design FMEA and especially the process FMEA?*

Q *Is the information on the control plans actually being used by shop personnel (should not be a paper exercise)?*

Q *Is there evidence that the control plans are living documents (which means more than just re-signing them once a year)?*

Q *Are the operators trained in using the information found in the control plans?*

7.5.1.2 Work instructions (Ford-Guidance)

Q *Are work instructions available for every operation in the plant (this can include office settings) and are they being used?*

Q *Is it evident that the work instructions are updated as changes in the process are made?*

Q *How is preventive action incorporated into the work instructions?*

Q *Are there too many work instructions in some of the work areas?*

Q *Work instructions should add value, not clutter, to the work areas!*

Q *Do some of the work instructions belong in the training manual?*

7.5.1.3 Verification of job setups
(Ford-Guidance)

Q *Is statistical information used for job setups in your plant?*

Note that the "where applicable" gives some flexibility, but does require data analysis in most cases! Thus, just having an engineer or manager say "we can do that here" is not satisfactory! If a process had been running in a stable (in control) condition before, how do the setup personnel know that they have reset the machine, tools, line, and so on, in the same way as before? Due to variation, checking one or two pieces is not acceptable any longer!

7.5.1.4 Preventive and predictive maintenance *
(Ford-Guidance)

Q *What is the efficiency of machines and operations in the shop?*

Q *How are data analyzed to predict when maintenance needs to be performed?*

Q *How is the typical overcollection of information being analyzed to help in predictive maintenance?*

Q *Are operators asked to help identify trends or patterns in the machines or lines?*

Q *Are key machines identified and monitored?*

Q *Is statistical data available for at least the key machines in the plant?*

7.5.1.5 Management of production tooling * (DCX-GM)

Q *Have any customer (internal or external) complaints had a root cause traceable to the design, fabrication, or verification of production tools or gages?*

Q *Is there a tracking system for internal problems?*

Q *What in the system* (never people) *allowed these issues to arise?*

Q *What steps are taken to prevent problems with tools or gages?*

With the seven items listed in the standard, the internal auditor should in essence be looking for an advanced quality plan for production tools and gages.

Q *How is the system working?*

Q *Is production tooling that is being stored at your facility (tools not being used for current production, maybe service part tools) being properly cared for, following the same requirements as current production tools?*

Note: The only time a production tool can be scrapped is when the customer provides scrap authorization. Thus, internal auditors need to look through some old records to see what production tools were used and see if tooling scrap authorization has been received. If not, then the tools need to be maintained!

7.5.1.6 Production scheduling

Q *How well does the quick changeover work in your plant (a source of many complaints by production personnel)?*

Q *Are the production scheduling, preventive maintenance, manufacturing supervision, and other related groups all taken into consideration when production schedules are set (this goes beyond just setting the daily schedule at a morning production meeting)?*

Q *How is advance planning being used?*

Q *What have been the results of measures relating to providing product to customers just in time?*

Q *Are late shipments an issue at your plant?*

7.5.1.7 Feedback of information from service *

The old practice of waiting for the customer to complain before taking any action is *no longer acceptable* in the automotive industry!

Q *How is your organization using proactive and preventive techniques to look for possible issues before they become problems with your parts?*

Q *Does your plant contact local automotive repair groups (automotive distribution outlets, service stations, dealerships, other vehicle repair organizations) to seek information about the parts produced in your plant?*

Q *What other methods is top management using to understand how the business impacts society? (This could possibly go beyond the production parts to environmental issues.)*

7.5.1.8 Service agreement with customer *

Q *Does your organization have any service agreements (which could mean shipping parts to service centers) with any of your customers?*

Q *If so, what is the process effectiveness in relationship to customer satisfaction?*

7.5.2 Validation of processes for production and service provision (Ford)

The term "in-vehicle position" describes the positioning of a part as it is used in the vehicle. The internal auditor needs to verify that all testing related to functional use is conducted in true vehicle position!

Q *How are all parts being produced and function-checked for validity purposes beyond the requirements found in the PPAP process?*

Q *What process is used to look for possible deficiencies that might occur in the future?*

Q *How are the concepts of prevention and usability being studied in the design and manufacturing process?*

Q *Does the process FMEA include these items?*

7.5.2.1 Validation of processes for production and service provision—Supplemental

See previous clause.

7.5.3 Identification and traceability (Ford-Guidance)

Q *How is product status marked (tagged) and identified at all stages in the plant?*

Q *Is there any chance of any materials (nonconforming or otherwise) being used without authorization or approval?*

Q *Is traceability marking up to date and accurate?*

Q *Can materials used be tracked to identify what was used in any given shipment to customers?*

Q *How are the identification and traceability factors measured in the plant?*

Q *How do the trends help to identify customer satisfaction?*

7.5.3.1 Identification and traceability— Supplemental

See previous clause.

7.5.4 Customer property (Ford)

Internal auditors should look at their organizations for anything that is owned by customers!

Q *How is this property being identified and maintained in the plant?*

Q *Are old tools available until written scrap authorization is received?*

Q *How are records of this property maintained?*

Q *Does this property have any impact on customer satisfaction for your plant?*

7.5.4.1 Customer-owned production tooling *

Q *Is all customer-owned property (usually tools) permanently marked with the customer's name?*

7.5.5 *Preservation of product (Ford)*

Q *Does any customer feedback indicate damage to product upon receipt at their facility?*

Q *If so, then what is happening in the process to allow such damage?*

Q *What steps are top managers taking to improve the product prior to customer use?*

7.5.5.1 *Storage and inventory (Ford-Guidance)*

Q *Is product stored for long periods in the plant rechecked periodically to ensure usability?*

Q *Is FIFO (first-in-first-out), LIFO (last-in-first-out), or FISH (first-in-still-here) being used?*

Q *If stored parts become obsolete, how are they labeled and handled?*

Q *How are the data from inventory turns measured by top management?*

Q *What plans are in place to improve the inventory turn in the plant?*

7.6 Control of monitoring and measuring devices

Q *Does the APQP process used at your plant include identification of a measurement plan and verification of that plan?*

Q *Are there resources available (human and equipment) to fulfill the requirements of the control plans?*

Q *Are all equipment specifications and practices being followed according to gage manufacturer recommendations or requirements?*

Q *Have any customer complaints or concerns been traced back to the measurement system?*

Q *If so, what preventive steps is top management taking to prevent future issues?*

Q *Is the MSA manual being followed (see 7.6.1)?*

Q *Do records show that the measurement system is effective in meeting customer requirements and satisfaction needs?*

Q *If software is used to track the measurement system, how was it validated prior to being used in the plant (just because the producer said it would work is not good enough)?*

7.6.1 Measurement system analysis * (Ford)

It is expected that the MSA manual is being followed unless a written customer authorization is provided as to alternatives!

Q *Is stability (control charts) being checked on at least one gage from each gage family?*

Q *Have full bias and linearity studies been done on at least one gage from each gage family?*

Q *If a particular gage becomes suspect for some reason, is it checked for full stability, bias, linearity, and gage repeatability and reproduceability with full graphical analysis?*

Q *Are "master parts" available for each stage of the production operation in which to run stability and other statistical analysis studies?*

Q *Are these master parts being handled and stored in a way to prevent deterioration?*

Q *What is being done to reduce the amount of variation in the measurement process?*

7.6.2 Calibration/verification records

Q *Are all gages used to make product included in the calibration system?*

Q *How are any new gages quarantined until being incorporated into the system?*

The internal auditor needs to be aware of the six items called out in the standard.

Q *How does the calibration system support customer satisfaction?*

Q *Do any customer complaints have a root cause in the calibration system?*

Q *What is top management doing to reduce variation in the calibration system and to demonstrate continual improvement of the measurement system?*

7.6.3 Laboratory requirements * (Ford)

7.6.3.1 Internal laboratory

The internal lab at your plant has to be treated as a mini-unit within the plant, thus the internal auditor will need to treat this group differently to ensure that the lab meets customer's expectations.

Q *Is the scope listed in the QMS, and how does it support the plant's drive for customer satisfaction?*

Q *Has ISO 17025 been used as a model for the laboratory?*

Q *If not, how is the process run to be in conformance (this word is appropriated for the lab) with standard lab operations?*

Q *Have needs assessments been done for the laboratory personnel that go beyond that done for production personnel?*

Q *Who handles lab personnel qualifications and are they clearly stated and up to date?*

7.6.3.2 External laboratory (Ford)

Q *Do all external laboratories have a defined scope on file with your plant?*

Q *Are they registered to ISO 17025 or have written approval for use by any customers impacted by the lab's service?*

Q *How are external labs selected and monitored to ensure that your plant's customer satisfaction is maintained related to the lab's services?*

8.0 MEASUREMENT, ANALYSIS AND IMPROVEMENT

8.1 General

Many top management groups try to manage the business through tables of numbers. They typically say that there is too much information to try to chart or graph what is happing in the business. If this is happening in your organization, then write a PAR on your top management for not analyzing and improving the effectiveness of the quality management system! How can people manage information by looking at a table of numbers? They cannot! Thus, top management must find a way to chart or graph the most important aspects of the business. This should then be cascaded down through management, staff, and operators to each chart or graph the most important aspects of each job! This is what is needed to incorporate statistical techniques throughout the organization. Remember the old adage: "Those who say it can't be done should get out of the way of those doing it!"

8.1.1 Identification of statistical tools (Ford)

Q *What statistical tools (we are not talking SPC or gages here) are being used in the various operations of the organization?*

Again, as in 8.1, top management is to ensure that all operations in the organization are using statistical techniques to manage the business and identify areas for improvement.

Q *Is it evident that the APQP process identified statistical tools that followed down into the paperwork and ended up on the control plans?*

8.1.2 Knowledge of basic statistical concepts * (Ford)

In one sentence, a large volume of understanding is being required! Example: if operators are allowed to change the settings of the process (for example, at the start of their shifts) without appropriate statistical direction, then the process is being overadjusted and the result will be at least a doubling of the variation in the process.

Q *Are people trained in understanding statistical applications? (Note: this is* not *just SPC.)*

Q *How is top management encouraging the use of appropriate statistical thinking?*

The internal auditors must know a lot about statistical techniques to be able to judge the use of such techniques within your organization! Thus, if your organization has not given you adequate training or experience, you will need to seek outside learning for understanding. You might want to contact your local ASQ section or visit ASQ's Web site, www.asq.org, as a starting point.

8.2 Monitoring and measurement

8.2.1 Customer satisfaction (new)

Sending out paper/e-mail surveys or hearing that the corporate office is handling this item does *not* meet the intent of this element!

Q *How is top management actively seeking information from internal and external customers and using statistical information to ensure that satisfaction is being achieved?*

8.2.1.1 Customer satisfaction—Supplemental * (DCX-Ford-GM-Guidance)

Please note that this item has high focus in every aspect of the standard support documents! In many cases, this information should be the starting point of internal audits to evaluate how the system is operating and the effectiveness of the system to ensure customer satisfaction. Data for the four items listed in this section (delivery, disruptions, schedules, notifications) are typically collected, and the internal auditor must ask:

Q *How is the information being statistically analyzed?*

The metrics listed in the standard (clause 8.2.1.1) should be considered as a minimum.

Q *The internal auditor needs to ask what else is being studied, using statistical analysis (versus just columns of data), to ensure customer satisfaction?*

Sometimes the people in the shipping department have a wealth of information (as they typically talk with customers on a daily basis), which is not always accessed by top management.

Charts and graphs should be available for these data and trends should be clear as to meeting or exceeding customer expectations! The internal auditor needs to be ready to question everyone about their understanding of these data and how their jobs impact the data. Thus, instead of just asking if someone knows the quality policy, you might ask:

Q *How does the customer information on this chart / graph impact how you use the company's quality policy in doing your job?*

8.2.2 Internal audit (Ford)

This is one of the clauses requiring a documented procedure.

Q *How does this process contribute to customer satisfaction?*

Q *Is the entire organization being audited at least once annually?*

Q *Has the audit frequency changed over the years and on what information have the changes been made? (The author has noted that due to the lagging economy in the United States over the last couple of years, audits have been scaled back due to lack of resources—this is not acceptable.)*

Q *Have the internal audits that have been done been correlated to increased customer satisfaction?*

The internal audit program should be one of top management's tools in ensuring that the entire organization is effectively satisfying customers (internal and external).

The audit program is to be planned and executed with the view of improving customer satisfaction. To that end, there should be evidence that top management has directed additional audits where needed as issues arise. If the audit manager is only conducting audits to the planned schedule, then there might be an issue of how top management is using or not using the internal audit program to improve the effectiveness of the organization. To this end, top management investigations should be included in the internal audit findings and, in some organizations, some top managers are themselves internal auditors.

When findings for corrective or preventive actions are identified, does top management respond to the items in a timely manner? Improvement should be seen throughout the organization and the internal audit program should be one of the key drivers for verifying that improvement will sustain the gains made by the organization.

8.2.2.1 Quality management system audit (Guidance)

Q *What correlation do the audit results show with the current international standards?*

Q *What other requirements are identified in the organization's goals to achieve customer satisfaction?*

Q *These requirements could either be internal organization items (from your plant or a corporate office) or directly from external customers.*

8.2.2.2 Manufacturing process audit * (Guidance)

The effectiveness called for here is giving the customers what they ask for and need.

Q *Does the plant have a proactive system of collecting information from customers to indicate how well your organization is satisfying the customers?*

This could also be applied to internal customers. A high internal ppm could be an indication of poor internal customer satisfaction.

8.2.2.3 Product audit (Guidance)

The internal auditor must try to understand the area process flowcharts (maps) to try to identify "appropriate stages of production." The idea is to look at areas with a questioning eye and ask if there is a better way of monitoring this area. In many cases, if the inspection is done only at the end of production, then waste is in the system! The top management is allowing product to be made before inspection. Prevention indicates that parameters need to be found that will help ensure that only good product is produced. The internal auditor's job is to identify possible areas for investigation or future study through the PAR.

8.2.2.4 Internal audit plans (Guidance)

Q *Does the internal audit program (and records of past audits) show that all shifts and areas have been included in the audit process?*

Q *Is an annual plan being utilized and have qualified auditors been assigned to the audits?*

Q *Do audit frequencies match up with customer ppm trends (that is, if the ppm increases, then internal audits should increase also)?*

8.2.2.5 Internal auditor qualifications (GM-Guidance)

Q *Are internal auditors qualified on the basis of appropriate training and / or experience for each audit completed?*

Q *What program is in place to continually improve the effectiveness of internal auditors?*

8.2.3 Monitoring and measurement of processes

This might be a difficult area for many internal auditors, as they will need to question engineers and top management as to the effectiveness of the overall measurement system. The basic saying here should be: "If we always do what we have always done, then we will always get what we always got!" Start by looking again at the overall trend of customer satisfaction over a multiyear period. Is it stable? If the trend is not in a positive direction, it could be a sign (but not a given) that the method of measurement is no longer adequate to accomplish what is being studied. This holds true for mechanical instruments as well as other measurement systems. The internal auditor may need to seek out measurement expertise, either in his or her own organization or outside, to ensure that the current measurement system that is in place is adequate.

8.2.3.1 Monitoring and measurement of manufacturing processes * (Ford-Guidance)

Here is another large section that the internal auditor will need to pay close attention to.

Q *Throughout the entire APQP process, does information flow and is information used to prevent problems in the manufacturing process and to support customer satisfaction?*

Many organizations either pay little attention to, or because of the number of people involved over the entire development process, lose track of what information is obtained during the various phases of product design, process design, product validation, process validation, prototype, PPAP, production, and closeout of products. Your organization may have different terms for these phases; however, your challenge is to identify how the information is being used to ensure continual improvement of customer satisfaction during the entire lifecycle of a part at the plant.

To assist the internal auditor in this clause, it is suggested that you ensure that you have reviewed the items listed in the five automotive core tool manuals (APQP, PPAP, FMEA, SPC, and MSA). As the internal auditor ensures the organization's effectiveness to meet customer needs and wants, each area of the organization that deals with getting a product to the customer (from initial sales contact to receiving scrap authorization for tools) is reviewed.

8.2.4 Monitoring and measurement of product (Ford)

Q *Are all customer-required measurements, as well as internally identified characteristics, being monitored in an effective manner to prevent nonconforming product from reaching the customer?*

8.2.4.1 Layout inspection and functional testing (Ford)

As required in PPAP, organizations must conduct a full layout inspection of all parts produced at your organization. There must also be records of supplier layouts that impact your organization's products. Remember that DCX suppliers must perform an annual layout per the DCX Customer Specific Requirements. Functional testing must be performed to simulate in-vehicle position during all testing. (That is, a door handle in a salt spray booth must be in a position to simulate how it would be exposed to moisture dripping down from the window.)

8.2.4.2 Appearance items (Ford)

If your product involves appearance items, then there are additional aspects of inspection that must be tracked and maintained for customer satisfaction. For MSA issues, protection must be available to prevent deterioration or discoloration of parts. Inspection masters must also be protected against negative environment factors.

8.3 Control of nonconforming product (Ford)

Please note the word used here is "nonconforming" product. Some organizations are also using the word "discrepancies." Either would be acceptable; however, within the automotive industry, the word "defect" is *not* acceptable due to product liability laws in the United States. If your organization is unintentionally using the word "defect," you should identify this as a major nonconformance!

Q *If someone in your organization finds a product that does not meet the customer specification, what is done?*

Q *Are procedures in place to prevent nonconforming product from actually reaching the customer?*

Q *Does nonconforming product ever reach the customer?*

Q *If you find that the answer to each of these three questions is yes, then there is something wrong!*

There is room for preventive action to be taken if customers are getting bad product from your organization. Please note that customers do change their minds sometimes and/or the assembly plants may have needs that were not identified by the customer engineering. These issues should have been caught during your APQP, so if managers try that excuse, then write up a nonconforming APQP process!

8.3.1 Control of nonconforming product—Supplemental

Parts must be marked or identified at all times during your process. Thus, from the incoming area all the way through to shipping, materials must be identified as to their usefulness or state in which that material is or is not to be used.

Q *If unlabeled material or parts are found in your plant, do people understand what to do?*

8.3.2 Control of reworked product

Q *If material is identified for rework, is it inspected and/or tested to ensure that the material will now meet the customer intent?*

A potential area for preventive action might be in tracking reworked material. It has been found that any time reworked material is allowed back into a system, it is those parts that cause concerns or problems for the customer.

Q *Is your rework causing a higher percentage of customer rejects? Do you know?*

8.3.3 Customer information

Q *Does your organization have a mechanism in place to notify a customer if nonconforming product is found after it has been shipped?*

This used to be considered heresy by many old plant personnel, but today it is a requirement of doing business in the automotive industry. The challenge is to prevent nonconforming material in the first place so that you do not need to tell the customer bad news. Now, if rejects should occur that cause delays or other concerns to your customers, your plant must make the first phone call (e-mail) to fix the problem.

8.3.4 Customer waiver * (Ford)

This requirement is also very difficult for many manufacturing groups to live up to. If nonconforming product is found and a waiver is requested, manufacturing must stop immediately until such authorization is obtained. But is this done, especially on the off shifts?

Q *Do the records in your plant identify when problems first occurred and what sequence was followed to correct the issue or to gain a waiver from the customer?*

Many plants have a tendency to continue running the parts and seek permission later. This practice is no longer acceptable!

8.4 Analysis of data

Everyone in the plant must be able to analyze basic information relating to his or her job. There are four basic categories listed in this requirement. Some organizations have started using score boards (balanced scorecards) at various points in the plant that might include items as: safety, quality, delivery, cost, morale, and/or environment (the acronym used is SQDCME). The internal auditor should ask questions of plant personnel to ensure understanding of the data.

8.4.1 Analysis and use of data *

Any trend that is not going in the direction that top management wants should be viewed as an opportunity for preventive action! Data should be viewed over time, not necessarily the current year. A common practice is to use a bar chart for the current year information with averages from the previous year or two. This is a very poor way to view data, especially in the early part of a year in question. It would be much better to show a run chart with 12 to 24 data points from the preceding months. This would allow for trend analysis or even an individual moving range chart. And yes, out-of-control points need to be addressed by top management!

Many plants actually are drowning in data! The internal auditor should be ready to collect this data whenever information is being tracked and create run charts or even control charts to replace pie or bar charts. Data can usually be displayed in many ways that can be appropriate, with the internal auditor looking for better ways to improve customer satisfaction. This is an area that internal auditors are encouraged to learn about as much as they can to be able to help everyone understand data better.

8.5 Improvement

8.5.1 Continual improvement (Ford)

Q *What mechanism(s) does your plant have to demonstrate that the QMS is being continually improved?*

Q *Do the explanations by all top managers and other managers agree with one another?*

Q *Are the trends positive?*

Q *How might the overall process (which may include communication) be improved?*

Q *Who is working on what?*

Q *The internal auditor may wish to study the Kano model to understand this requirement better!*

8.5.1.1 Continual improvement of the organization (Guidance)

Q *Does the top management (versus the quality representative) have a process in place to ensure that continual improvement to satisfaction of customer wants and needs is actually happening?*

8.5.1.2 Manufacturing process improvement *

Q *Is evidence of waste reduction present for manufacturing operations?*

Q *Are error-proofing and other techniques of preventing waste (muda) effective in improving customer satisfaction?*

Q *What is manufacturing doing to prevent future problems?*

8.5.2 Corrective action (Ford)

This is one of the clauses requiring a documented procedure. It specifically looks at what was done when things have gone wrong.

Q *How does this process contribute to customer satisfaction?*

Q *What is being done if and when issues arise on the shop floor, shipping, or anywhere else?*

The internal auditor program needs to aggressively study these items to assist top management in understanding the plant process better.

8.5.2.1 Problem solving (Guidance)

There are a number of problem-solving models available.

Q *How is your organization ensuring that personnel are trained in and actually use the customer-prescribed technique to solve issues?*

Q *Are personnel throughout the plant and organization trained in using problem-solving techniques?*

8.5.2.2 Error-proofing (Guidance)

Q *Are personnel throughout the plant and organization trained in using error-proofing (mistake-proofing) techniques?*

Q *Has error-proofing been used to eliminate root causes of problems in the plant?*

8.5.2.3 Corrective-action impact *

Q *Once a root cause has been found and eliminated, have similar processes been reviewed to see if the same fix should be applied to those processes?*

Q *What records of results are available?*

8.5.2.4 Rejected product test/analysis * (Guidance)

Besides any formal channels that may exist with your customers (by the way, do you know what they are?), does top management seek other ways to gather customer information? One possible technique might be to visit your local dealerships to talk with vehicle technicians about parts that your plant produces. You might get some interesting pointers from these mechanics about how well your parts perform in the field.

Q *How is information gathered and used to improve the overall process (including development cycle time)?*

8.5.3 Preventive action (Ford)

This is one of the clauses requiring a documented procedure.

Q *How does this process contribute to customer satisfaction?*

It is easy to say that we practice prevention, but is this actually being done?

Q *Can the internal auditor show the number of corrective actions taken in the organization in comparison to the number of preventive actions taken?*

If prevention is being used properly, then there should be far more preventive actions for every corrective action taken. This also applies to the internal audit program itself! Internal auditors should find far more preventive actions for top managers to review instead of just corrective actions. You should become another set of eyes and ears to help the company to ensure that continual improvement of customer satisfaction is practiced daily.

ANNEX A—CONTROL PLAN

A.1 Phases of the control plan

- Prototype
- Prelaunch
- Production

Q *Are control plans available covering all three phases of the APQP process (gray box suppliers may not have a prototype control plan)?*

Q *Are cross-functional teams used to create and maintain the control plans? Is the APQP manual followed in development of control plans?*

A.2 Elements of the control plan

- General data
- Product control/process control/methods/ reaction plan and corrective action

Q *Are each of the items listed in the standard covered in the control plans?*

Q *How does the control plan help improve customer satisfaction?*

Q *How is top management working on the control plan to reduce variation in the products, processes, and timing for customer satisfaction?*

AUTOMOTIVE CORE TOOLS

Advance Product Quality Planning and Control Plan (APQP)

The APQP manual was developed to provide guidelines of what information is needed to launch a new product from a plant. One of the big concerns of the APQP development team was that many organizations assigned this task to the quality departments, but the quality people do not make anything. Thus the term "product" was added to the former term of AQP to indicate that the product engineers should be leading the charge of new product development. If your organization has the quality people leading this, then close review of the top management is needed.

Questions that could be asked include:

Q *Has the organization developed an APQP process specific to the needs of this plant? If not, how do they know when they have*

successfully completed the APQP process?
Note: Non-design plants still need to use
APQP to launch the product!

Q *Who manages the APQP process? Does this make sense for the conditions of your plant?*

Q *Are true cross-functional teams used (versus one person doing all the work)?*

Q *Is the process a living function with data being updated regularly?*

Q *Does top management include data from APQP as an input to the management review process?*

Production Part Approval Process

The *Production Part Approval Process* (PPAP) manual was always considered a standard (versus a reference manual as the other four core tool books). Thus, this manual has a number of "shall" statements that need to be complied with. Any exceptions to what is required in this manual must have written documentation to that fact from a controlling customer.

Questions that could be asked include:

Q *Are data available for all parts that have not received formal tool scrap authorization from the customer?*

Q *Are data in a retrievable format?*

Q *Are sample / master parts available and in a state as to prevent possible damage?*

Failure Mode and Effects Analysis

It has been demonstrated and proven that failure mode and effects analysis (FMEA) can and will help eliminate problems if used appropriately. Why then do so few organizations use this powerful tool to help prevent problems? Time seems to be the key factor for many groups. There is not enough time to do it right the first time, but there is enough time to do it over again! Top management must provide the resources to ensure that this tool is utilized in your plant.

Questions that could be asked include:

Q *Are true cross-functional teams used (versus one person doing all the work)?*

Q *Have plant-specific occurrence and detection tables been developed? If not, then the process will not work the way it is intended to!*

Q *Are design FMEAs available?*

Q *Have all process FMEAs been completed and are they current?*

Q *Have data from the FMEA been filtered down to control plans and work instructions?*

Q *Have there been past problems that the FMEA should have caught? What is top management doing to correct this issue?*

Q *How is the FMEA being used as a preventive tool?*

Statistical Process Control

Many organizations have used some version of statistical process control (SPC) for many years. There was a large push by the Big Three in the early 1980s to use statistical information. However, many plants got into the habit of doing statistical process display (SPD)—making charts, but not using them to evaluate the process. Today, there is a growing movement to call the charts process behavior charts. This points to the fact that the use of statistical data is useful in monitoring what a process is doing. Given the changeover to the process approach of top management and auditing, the plant needs to manage the process using statistical data that correlates to overall customer satisfaction.

Questions that could be asked include:

Q *Do all key processes (as identified by top management) have statistical process charts to monitor how the processes are doing?*

Q *Are the charts updated in real time and do operators have the tools and authority to make appropriate changes as indicated by the charts?*

Q *Are all data used to manage the business analyzed using appropriate statistical tools (just using bar charts may not be the most appropriate method of evaluating a process over time)?*

Q *Are trends, runs, patterns, or other nonrandom issues responded to in a timely and appropriate manner?*

Q *Is everyone in the organization trained to understand and use statistical information?*

Measurement Systems Analysis

With the release of the third edition of *Measurement Systems Analysis* (MSA), a new focus on measurement error has been established. This is primarily due to the fact that many plants have done a very good job of finding and eliminating the cause of variation on the production floor. Today, more and more variation of parts is due to measurement error, and the MSA design team felt that it was time to establish a continual improvement process for the measurement system. There is a new focus on identifying the stability, bias, linearity, and analysis of GR&R that was mentioned before but not enforced. Today, a lot more time, energy, and resources are needed to conduct MSA studies. If your plant does what it has always done, then the results will not be acceptable.

Questions that could be asked include:

Q *Have families of gages been identified?*

Q *Are master parts available for each part for the gaging requirements? (Note that these are not sample master parts and they must be protected from wear and other issues.)*

Q *Is at least one stability study being done for each family?*

Q *Has a bias and linearity study been done on each family?*

Q *Does the GR&R include a full graphical analysis as outlined in the manual?*

Q *What is being done to study the measurement error in your plant?*

Q *Are any data available to demonstrate continual improvement of the gaging system?*

8

Follow-Up

Internal auditors are not done with the audit process by just turning in their audit findings and hoping that top management will do the rest! In many cases, top management may make an adjustment or change something, then after a little break-in time, ask the same internal auditor(s) to recheck that area, department, or function to see if the improvement has worked. This is part of the follow-up process and it is important to keep good records so that future internal auditors will understand how the process has evolved.

ENVIRONMENTAL, HEALTH, AND SAFETY

Since all automotive suppliers to the U.S. automotive OEMs must be registered to ISO 14001, it will be common for internal auditors to watch for observations of environmental compliance. Also, with the developing ISO 18001, health and safety issues will likely be coming very soon to the automotive industry. Basically, the internal auditor should always be observant for possible safety issues that employees face in any process. Loose electrical cords, air hoses, or other objects left lying around on the floor can become health or safety hazards. Spills of liquids, especially in enclosed areas, can become dangerous environmental issues. There are any number of things that we tend to overlook because they have become so familiar to us.

The challenge to the internal auditors of the QMS is to be open-minded about everything around them so as not to overlook possible issues, and call them out as PARs for top management review. In this way, the internal audit programs can add a lot of unexpected value to an organization and possibly help to save someone's life or prevent injuries in the plant.

CORRECTIVE ACTION REPORTS

A number of corrective action report (CAR) programs have not made a significant impact on organizations. Problems may go away for some time, but eventually return. Once these issues return, enough time has passed that many have forgotten the issue ever happened and the whole process of problem solving starts all over again.

Real problem solving has not occurred until you have the "light switch" to the problem! That means the problem has been so well studied and recognized that the root cause can be turned on or off (like a light switch) and the problem comes or goes in direct relationship to changing the root cause. It is only at this point that root causes can truly be labeled and controlled to ensure that problems do not reach the customers.

Sporadic, irregular problems are the most difficult to discover the root causes of. By studying the process as a working system, we should be able to, over time, start discovering more of these sporadic events to give us a better opportunity in identifying and removing these root causes.

Another point to make in this section is to remind internal auditors that the CAR process needs to be updated with the focus on customer satisfaction. The old process had the internal auditor writing up every situation where people were not following the written procedure. Now, the first question that must be asked is whether the procedure leads to customer satisfaction! Thus, just because someone is not doing exactly what the procedure says does *not* immediately mean that the person is wrong. The procedure may be wrong given current customer wants! The internal auditor must judge whether the customer will receive better results if this alternate approach is continued. If the answer is yes, then a PAR (not a CAR) should be written against the procedure.

Top management will probably use internal auditing to verify that corrective actions have been effectively addressed and resolved. The challenge will be to ensure that with the resolution of concerns, customer satisfaction is actually improved.

PREVENTIVE ACTION REPORTS

Many organizations have typically included in the corrective action procedure a line including preventive action. However, in reality, very little was done to actually try to prevent issues from occurring. This is one of the areas that ISO/TS 16949:2002 is focusing on and that top management must now address to develop an actual preventive approach to problems in the organization. Many employees have ideas and suggestions, so a true employee suggestion program could be a good first step.

Internal auditors, as previously mentioned, will also need to address possible areas for improvement that are found during the internal audit through a preventive action report (PAR) process.

As with the CAR program, follow-up will be needed to ensure that each PAR that is written will be addressed in some format by top management.

A key item here is also the fact that it is expected that the internal audit program will be very rigorous and extensive. Top management is to review the results of the internal audit program as one of the inputs of management review, and external audits will be looking closely at how the PAR process has been implemented in the plant.

AUDIT CLOSURE

All internal audits should end with a closing meeting with the area supervisors and possibly top management. Then a written report should be assembled for filing and for the input of the top management reviews. The written report could include: copies of process maps (flowcharts), a list of measurables, check sheets used, turtle diagrams assembled (or other related forms), listings of any CARs and PARs, and any other findings/notes about the internal audit. The more detail the better, both for review by top management and for reference by future internal auditors.

Table 8.1 is designed to assist the internal auditor with ideas for evaluating the audit and the next step of following up on the CARs and PARs. A procedure to ensure that closure occurs on all

Table 8.1

	Evaluation and Follow-Up *(If appropriate)*
Questions for consideration	What information and results are important to the plant? What measurements are useful? What should be assessed to get at the information? How are the results going to be used? Are additional interventions required to achieve the desired result? Are the appropriate performance levels in place? Is the top management satisfied?
Auditing activities	If a team audit, share results with team Summarize and present findings at closing meeting Write up a final report Initiate preventive-action requests "PAR" Initiate corrective-action reports "CAR" If appropriate, follow up on PAR and CAR to closure
Organization considerations	Evaluate audit effectiveness Identify lessons learned so the next audit will be even better Look for personal continual improvement opportunities Celebrate achievements

continued

continued

	Evaluation and Follow-Up *(If appropriate)*
Pitfalls to avoid	No evaluation is done No one takes ownership of unsatisfactory results No corroboration on results Finding no opportunities for continual improvement Scope was cloudy Not agreeing on when PAR or CAR results should be expected
Potential tools	Final audit report Corrective action reports Preventive action report PAR/CAR follow-up matrix

items will need to be in place for your organization and an internal auditor should be asked to verify that items have been addressed.

SUMMARY

Special training is needed to become an environmental management system (EMS) internal auditor, however, every auditor should be aware of implications of environmental issues and stay alert to possible issues. As for the health and safety factor, an international standard is in development and should soon be available for use on the shop floor. Here also, internal auditors should keep an eye open for obvious or potential issues to be reported to top management. In either case, the PAR process should be used to ensure that no legal issues arise from an untrained internal auditor writing a CAR. If you have the appropriate training, then use it accordingly; otherwise, just inform management about a possible concern.

The CAR and PAR processes are important to the plant and are included in the IATF high-focus clauses. Internal auditors should use these as needed to draw attention to important items that top management needs to address. With the focus of ISO/TS 16949:2002 on customer satisfaction and continual improvement, many of the CARs and PARs should be directed with these concepts as the end result. Also, as was said, we are to be moving into a preventive mode, so there should be a developing pattern of far more PARs written during audits than CARs.

9

Automotive Case Studies

The basis of the following information is real. The names and situations have been slightly altered to provide anonymity for the plants involved.

CASE STUDY A: CASTING AREA

The casting department has 50 aluminum casting operations that run three shifts per day, seven days a week. Molten aluminum is trucked to the plant from a nearby foundry and is transferred to each casting operation as needed to maintain the prescribed level in the furnaces. Each operation consists of a press that cools the molten aluminum into a forged part and a furnace that is a large box with a lid that opens to receive the molten aluminum. Paddles ladle molten aluminum from the furnace as needed by the forging operation. Heating elements are built into the lid to maintain the aluminum at the desired temperature until used in the forging operation.

Twice during each shift, electricians visit each machine to ensure that the amperage draw is within prescribed tolerances for the furnace. Adjustments are made based on each reading. During the course of each week, each operator completes a log sheet of cleaning and operation of the forge/furnace. A preventive maintenance procedure is used to review each machine on a three-month cycle. A detailed maintenance log is maintained in a computer system and shows everything done to every machine in the plant.

During a typical element audit, the internal auditors would review the various logs to ensure that all paperwork was present in the appropriate locations. CARs were typically written for paperwork missing in the files.

What value added is the paperwork in this case? What and how should a process audit be conducted in this area?

Findings

1. There was no formal information from the next operation as to how good or poor the castings were!

2. Most of the operator weekly reports were present; however, a few were missing over a six-month period of review.

3. One machine was noticed to have a lot of operator comments about its operation. It "needed a new furnace." Over a six-month period, nearly every weekly report stated "needs new furnace," but no records were found to indicate that any work other than installation of new lids had actually been performed. The request was not on the preceding two weekly reports. The internal auditors questioned the operator on that machine and were told that a new furnace was finally installed about a week and a half before. No records could be found to support the operator observation.

4. The electrician reports were copied and turned in to the shift production supervisors. These reports sat on the supervisor's conference table for a day or two until someone decided to throw the old reports (several days old) out. The first report from the first shift was kept in a three-ring binder and the area foreman used this report of the 50 machines to make a generalization of how the area was running for the daily plant managers' meeting. A review of the preceding six months showed all reports available.

5. Preventive maintenance was on schedule. It was discovered under questioning during the

three-month reviews that only the forging equipment was checked as it was assumed that the electricians checked the furnaces daily.

6. Construction was being undertaken in an adjacent room that would redirect cooling ducts through this department along the shared wall. Some operators on machines along this wall were concerned about the furnaces being able to hold proper heat given the cool air movement in the area.

See report A in appendix A for actual write-ups on the casting area.

CASE STUDY B: ROLE PLAY OF CUSTOMER REJECTION

During the recent three-day audit, data were collected in shipping about recent parts that had been shipped in the past couple of days to particular customers. Then, one of those parts was checked to see what materials were used in making that part. Records were reviewed to check for traceability issues and other items of the overall system during a normal audit.

On the last morning of the audit, the auditor asked to talk with the the person responsible for handling customer complaints. As this person arrived with the audit coordinator, the auditor first said, "This is a test—*not* a real situation—only a drill!"

The scenario goes like this: Part # ___ which was shipped on date ___ has just been received by customer ABC. They are rejecting the entire shipment due to poor quality (used a basic issue typical to this plant found during the previous two days of auditing)! One issue involves component # ___ as it seems to be failing test ___. How are you going to respond to this customer? You have four hours to develop a response and initial an action plan!

Question: As the internal auditor, what might you be looking for? Before looking in the appendix, make a list of things that you would want to see from the reaction team.

The auditor asked for a working lunch to be arranged to allow for the response team (expecting more than one person to be involved in this issue) to report. Management was advised and invited to the noon meeting.

See report 2 in appendix A for possible items to look for and some of the findings of the auditor.

CASE STUDY C: INTERNAL AUDIT PROGRAM

During the normal course of an audit, the internal audit program is being reviewed.

Findings

1. Names of internal auditors found with indication that all but two meet current requirements.

2. One of those who did not meet requirements had transferred to a sister plant more than six months before. The other person had been absent from the plant on the days that the training was conducted to meet the ISO/TS 16949:2002 requirements.

3. A cycle of audits had been established to have internal auditors assigned to conduct monthly portions of audits to cover the entire organization for the current year.

4. Audit reports up through the prior month were found on file; however, looking over the reports revealed missing information or comments to the effect that everything was "OK." This was contrary to a number of findings of the external auditor during this visit (for example, MSA said OK, but this auditor found that the current system was to the second edition MSA manual that had been replaced more than a year prior by the third edition).

5. For the immediately preceding month, only two of six audit reports (due by the end of each month), were in the files. Only one of the other four reports was found, in the process of being

"reviewed." Three were not done yet, thus over-due. The audit coordinator stated that she had informed management about the missing reports, but *no* action had been taken to her knowledge and there was no word on when the reports would be forthcoming.

What should the internal auditor do? What are the nonconformities, if any?

See report 3 in appendix A for actual write-ups on the internal audit program.

10

Next Steps

For many organizations, the transition to a process approach takes some time to get used to and developing singular process maps for each area may take some effort. The next challenge that is facing many organizations is then to develop or identify the linkages between processes. The current linkages have evolved over time and top management must now look at what is occurring in practice and decide if that method optimizes the process or if there is room for continual improvement.

PRACTICE, PRACTICE, PRACTICE

Can this be said any more plainly? To become a good auditor, it takes study and practice. Working with people takes time and effort, especially becoming a good observer and listener. It has been said that we have been given two eyes, two ears, and one mouth—and we should use each in those proportions. The challenge for many of us is that in formal education, we rarely, if ever, receive training in good observation and especially in good listening techniques.

ADDITIONAL TRAINING
IF NEEDED

Internal auditors are responsible for identifying when they feel that they need additional training to be able to conduct audits better (internal auditor continual improvement). Staying current with changing standards and technologies is becoming an ever-increasing task. Today, with the Internet, distance learning, conferences (local and national), books, videos, audios, and other sources, the challenge to stay current (never mind expanding knowledge) has become a challenge.

The internal auditor is expected to stay current and improve his or her skills in conducting audits. As with all personnel in the organization, the pursuit of personal continual improvement applies across all processes, including the training process.

CERTIFICATION (INTERNAL VERSUS EXTERNAL)

Some companies use a certification process to ensure that the internal auditors meet minimum requirements to be on audit teams within their organizations. These internal certifications can take many forms, but usually have some aspect of a certain number of hours of training followed by practical application working with other internal auditors. Organizations that choose this approach are cautioned to ensure that they stay current with the automotive industry requirements. Currently the Ford Customer-Specific Requirements have the most technical content, but they may be accepted by other OEMs as the minimum requirements.

ASQ offers the primary external certification programs available today. These are professional certifications offered as peer recognition that a person has a base level of knowledge that has been identified by the Society as being needed in a particular field of endeavor.

The primary auditing certification offered by ASQ for auditors is called the Certified Quality Auditor (CQA). This exam is a five-hour, open-book exam offered at various times throughout the year and is open to anyone who can show eight years of work experience or formal education and work experience. The body of knowledge (BOK) in appendix C gives a list of what knowledge a candidate will need to study. Many ASQ sections provide local refresher courses to help people prepare for the exam.

For those who may not have enough experience to apply for the CQA, an exam called the Certified Quality Improvement Associate (CQIA) might be an option. This four-hour exam is open to anyone. The BOK is listed in appendix B.

QUALITY MANAGEMENT PRINCIPLES

ISO/TS 16949:2002 is built on eight basic quality management principles:

1. Customer focus

2. Leadership

3. Involvement of people

4. Process approach

5. System approach to management

6. Continual improvement

7. Factual approach to decision making

8. Mutually beneficial supplier relationships

The internal auditor should be able to see these principles used by top management in an ongoing effort to continually improve customer satisfaction and the overall optimization of your organization. Minutes of top management review meetings should contain many references to planning for improvement of the organization. The automotive OEMs are looking for suppliers throughout the supply chain to be excellent suppliers always looking for improvements and pushing hard to move forward. As one major tier-one company likes to advertise, organizations and internal auditors must seek relentless improvement.

CONCLUSION

This book was designed to be an aid for automotive internal auditors while they are conducting audits within their organizations. To that end, tips and ideas have been put forward to aid the internal auditor while on the shop floor or in an office. Given the size limitations of this format, not every aspect of automotive internal auditing was covered here. But it is hoped that enough automotive-specific items have been covered to spark ideas as auditors progress with their activities.

It is also hoped that through this offering, the practice of automotive internal auditing will be moved forward under the process approach and that top managers will see a value added to ISO/TS 16949:2002 that has been missing in previous automotive standards.

If you would like to make comments to the author about this book or suggest ideas for continual improvement of this material, please email authors@asq.org. We would like to hear how this helps in your auditing process.

Thank you and good auditing.

Appendix A

Analysis of Case Studies

CASTING AREA

The casting area has a number of opportunities for improvement. During the old element-based audit, the internal auditor used to only review the paperwork to ensure that the local procedures were being followed. However, with the process audit approach, they were instructed to think very differently about how the operation was actually running. In this case, there were no obvious customer data—this is a PAR under 4.1.f. Without knowing what the next operation or ultimate user of the casting thought about this department's output, how do they know if they are moving on the right track?

The foreman only used one of the six reports that the electricians submitted each day to WAG about the operation of the area. This too is a PAR under 8.1.2, as no analysis of these data was being conducted. The internal auditors took the previous six-month reports for the target machine to show that the furnace was not in a state of statistical control.

The target furnace was reviewed in all of the available data logs, and no records of a new furnace were found even though there was in fact a new "rebuilt" furnace at the machine. A PAR under 7.5.1.4 was written as everyone knew that the computer database was not kept up to date and that many repairs done to machines were never recorded.

The internal auditors were able to identify that new lids had been put on the target furnace four times over the preceding six months, which was considered a high number of rebuilds. No record of the furnace was ever found, but the best guess of the internal auditors and production supervisor was that the last lid change occurred a couple of days before the furnace was changed. Once a furnace is changed, the entire box including the lid is pulled and rebuilt! That meant that the last recorded lid replacement, at a cost of several thousand dollars, was totally wasted given the installation of the rebuilt furnace.

There are other items that could have been written for this area, but given the wasted cost that was identified, the audit manager wanted to go with the aforementioned to demonstrate to the plant manager the value of changing over to this new process auditing approach. The plant manager agreed and requested that all further audits at that plant be of the process approach nature.

ROLE PLAY OF CUSTOMER REJECTION—CASE SCENARIO

In this scenario, a part is chosen that has been recently shipped and a simulated customer rejection is initiated. What is the plant going to do?

The first time this was used on an auditee, the results were basically good with a few PARs identified in the way materials were tracked by the information technology group; however, one thing did develop that generated a CAR.

- Most of the components that went into the part could be traced to within about a half day of production time. One screw, however, could not be identified to within a week! It was not felt that this screw would cause any real issues with the parts, thus it was not considered to be very important.

- The plant was able to pinpoint that if the supposed faulty component was in fact the issue, it came from a shipment that was used on four shifts of production.

- A number of these parts were still in the plant, so they could be quarantined.

- To cover customer ABC, a local inspection house could be contacted and working on the parts within an hour and additional parts could be sent as more stock was on the floor having been produced with supposed good components. If suspect parts were identified, then those would have to be returned for further testing and possible repair.

- As fresh stock was available, if needed, air and ground shipments could have new parts at customer ABC within 12 hours.

- It turned out that two other customers also received this part, but neither of these customers had received any suspect product. So, no further action was warranted with them.

- A plant representative could be dispatched immediately with new components to replace the suspect part at customer ABC to augment the inspection that would be started.

- The investigation team felt that the best course of action would include:

- Sending the local inspection company into customer ABC to start sorting (within one hour).

- Sending a engineer to customer ABC for further investigation.

- Opening lines of communication with customer ABC to keep them up to date on covering production and corrective actions.

• The company's quality manual and procedures that cover ISO/TS 16949:2002 6.3.2 Contingency Plans had no allowance for "key equipment failure and field returns." The plant did respond well to this scenario and thus a CAR was not written. What saved them in this situation was having additional stock on hand that could be used.

The cross-functional investigation team (quality, production, and purchasing) did a good job of investigating and coming up with fixes for the situation presented to them. The team leader even was overheard saying, "That was a lot easier than I expected when we started!" However, if a major problem had been detected with a component of the part, there was no planning on how to cover the customer. Thus, a CAR was written against top management for lack of planning in Contingency Plans 6.3.2.

INTERNAL AUDITOR PROGRAM

It is the responsibility of the top management to ensure that the internal audit program works as a value-added process for the plant. In this case, it appeared that the internal auditor program was used as a method to check off a box that an internal audit was done.

1. *Names of internal auditors on a list.* This by itself may not be an issue if those on the list who are not currently qualified have not done an audit or may be in training with other qualified internal auditors.

2. *Person who transferred out.* Could be overlooked and say to just remove the name. The other person should only be used as an on-the-job internal auditor until he or she meets full requirements.

3. *A cycle of audits had been established.* This meets the requirements.

4. *Audit reports were not complete and items reported were to old standards* (MSA, second edition). A CAR was issued against the top management, as this should have been caught during their management reviews. Thus, there could have actually been two issues that do not meet ISO/TS 16949:2002 (internal audits not complete and management reviews).

5. *Recent reports not turned in.* This generated the second CAR against the internal auditor program for lack of auditor knowledge as well as the program not being up to date with the annual cycle plan.

There were a number of areas where this program could be improved, and it was suggested that top management needed to do a formal review of their internal auditor programs. This, in fact, was a PAR for top management.

Appendix B

ASQ Certified Quality Improvement Associate— Body of Knowledge

I. Quality Basics
    A. Terms, Concepts, and Principles
        1. Quality
        2. Systems and processes
        3. The importance of employees
        4. Quality planning
        5. Variation
    B. Benefits of Quality
    C. Quality Philosophies
        1. Deming (14 points)
        2. Juran (Trilogy)
        3. Crosby (Zero defects)
II. Teams
    A. Types of Teams
        1. Improvement teams
        2. Cross-functional teams
        3. Project teams
        4. Self-directed teams

    B. Roles and Responsibilities
    C. Team Formation and Group Dynamics
        1. Initiating teams
        2. Selecting team members
        3. Group-think
        4. Team stages
III. Continuous Improvement
    A. Incremental and Breakthrough
       Improvement
    B. Improvement Cycles
    C. Quality Improvement Tools
    D. Customer–Supplier Relationships
        1. Internal and external customers
        2. Customer feedback
        3. Internal and external supplier
        4. Supplier feedback

Appendix C

ASQ Certified Quality Auditor—Body of Knowledge

I. Auditing Fundamentals
   A. Basic terms and concepts
   B. Purpose of audits
   C. Types of quality audits
   D. Audit criteria
   E. Roles and responsibilities of audit participants
   F. Ethical, legal, and professional issues
      1. Audit credibility
      2. Liability issues
      3. Professional conduct and responsibilities

II. Audit Process
   A. Audit preparation and planning
      1. Elements of the audit planning process
      2. Auditor selection
      3. Audit-related documentation
      4. Logistics

Appendix D

Resources

WEB SITES

www.aiag.org
Automotive Industry Action Group
Lists the current core tool manuals and plans to list the customer-specific requirements for major tier-one companies.

www.asq.org
American Society for Quality
Many items related to quality control, quality assurance, and other related issues concerning the field of continual improvement.

www.astd.org
American Society for Training and Development
Professional society dealing in training and training effectiveness.

www.iaob.org
International Automotive Oversight Bureau
Current policies and procedures to be used by registrars and the latest U.S. OEM customer-specific requirements.

www.insidequality.com
Inside Quality
Summaries of things happening in quality, Six Sigma, and other continual improvement initiatives.

www.iso.ch/iso/en/ISOOnline.openerpage
International Organization for
  Standardization (ISO)
ISO standards and related information.

www.ispi.org
International Society for Performance
  Improvement
Professional society dealing in training and training effectiveness.

www.ramquniverse.com
RAM Q Universe, Inc.
Business improvement methodologies.

Glossary and Acronyms

GLOSSARY

bench audit—An audit conducted at a desk reviewing the paper trail.

black box—Designation for suppliers who have part design responsibility.

external customer—The person or organization that will receive the output of your plant's production.

grey box—Designation for suppliers who only manufacture parts—*no* design responsibility.

internal customer—The person or department that will receive the output of your cell or department's work on the parts.

ACRONYMS

AIAG—Automotive Industry Action Group

ANFIA—Italian equivalent to the AIAG

APQP—advance product quality planning

ASTD—American Society for Training and Development

BOK—body of knowledge

COP—customer-oriented process

CQA—Certified Quality Auditor

CQIA—Certified Quality Improvement Associate

DCX—DaimlerChrysler Corporation

FIEV—French equivalent to the AIAG

FMEA—failure mode and effects analysis

GR&R—gage repeatability and reproducibility

IATF—International Automotive Task Force

IAOB—International Automotive Oversight Bureau

ISO—International Organization for Standardization

ISPI—International Society for Performance Improvement

KCDS—Key Characteristics Designation System (GM-specific)

MSA—measurement systems analysis

OSHA—Occupational Safety and Health Administration

PDCA—plan–do–check–act

PDSA—plan–do–study–act

PPAP—production part approval process

PSO—part sign-off (Chrysler-specific)

QFD—quality function deployment

QMS—quality management system

QS—quality systems requirements

QSA—quality system assessment

QSU—quality system update

SMMT—British equivalent to the AIAG

SPEAR—Suppler Performance and Evaluation Report (GM-specific)

SPC—statistical process control

SQA—supplier quality assurance

SQDCME—safety, quality, delivery, cost, morale, and environment

SQE—supplier quality engineer

SQI—supplier quality improvement (Ford-specific)

SQRTF—Supplier Quality Requirements Task Force

STA—supplier technical assistance (Ford-specific)

TIR—traceability identifier equipment (GM-specific)

TNA—training needs assessment

TS—technical specification

VDA—German equivalent to the AIAG

Bibliography

AIAG. 2002. *Automotive Certification Scheme for ISO/TS 16949:2002—Rules for Achieving IATF Recognition.* www.aiag.org/publications/quality/iatfquality.asp.

AIAG. 2002. *IATF Guidance to ISO/TS 16949:2002.* www.aiag.org/publications/quality/iatfquality.asp.

AIAG. 2002. *Quality System Assessment Checklist—Checklist to ISO/TS 16949:2002.* www.aiag.org/publications/quality/iatfquality.asp.

Arter, D. R., C. A. Cianfrani, and J. E. West. 2003. *How to Audit the Process-Based QMS.* Milwaukee: ASQ Quality Press.

Benbow, D. W., R. W. Berger, A. K. Elshennawy, and H. F. Walker. 2002. *The Certified Quality Engineer Handbook.* Milwaukee: ASQ Quality Press.

DaimlerChrysler. 2003. DaimlerChrysler Customer Specific Requirements (February): www.iaob.org/oem_req.html.

Ford Motor Company. 2003. *Ford Motor Company Customer Specific Requirements* (October): www.iaob.org/oem_req.html.

General Motors. 2003. *General Motors Customer Specific Requirements* (October): www.iaob.org/oem_req.html.

Marash, S. A., P. Berman, and M. Flynn. 2003. *Fusion
     Management: Harnessing the Power of Six Sigma,
     Lean, ISO 9001:2000, Malcolm Baldrige, TQM and
     Other Quality Breakthroughs of the Past Century.*
     Fairfax, VA: QSU Publishing Company.
Russell, J.P. 2003. *The Internal Auditing Pocket Guide.*
     Milwaukee: ASQ Quality Press.
———. 2003. *The Process Auditing Techniques Guide.*
     Milwaukee: ASQ Quality Press.
Smith, R. D., R. A. Munro, and R. J. Bowen. 2004. *The ISO/TS
     16949:2002 Answer Book.* Chico, CA: Paton Press.
Stimson, W. A. 2001. *Internal Quality Auditing: Meeting the
     Challenge of ISO 9000:2000.* Chico, CA: Paton Press.

QUALITY AUDITOR CERTIFICATION (CQA) REFERENCES

These books cover the parts of the body of knowledge. The ASQ Certification Board does not endorse any one particular reference source.

ANSI/ASQC. 1994. ANSI/ASQC Q10011-1994 Series,
     Guidelines for Auditing Quality Systems. Milwaukee:
     ASQC Quality Press.
Arter, D. R. 1994. *Quality Audits for Improved
     Performance,* Second ed. Milwaukee: ASQC Quality Press.
———. 2003. *Quality Audits for Improved Performance,* Third
     ed. Milwaukee: ASQ Quality Press.
ASQ Quality Audit Division, Russell, J.P. ed. 2000.
     The Quality Audit Handbook, Second ed. Milwaukee:
     ASQ Quality Press, 2000.

Brassard, M. and D. Ritter. 1994. *The Memory Jogger II.*
    Goal/QPC.

Federow, H. L. 1997. *Quality Practices and the Law.*
    Productivity Press.

Gryna, F. 2001. *Quality Planning and Analysis: From
    Product Development through Use,* Fourth ed. New York:
    McGraw-Hill.

Ishikawa, K. 1986. *Guide to Quality Control.* White Plains,
    NY: Quality Resources.

Juran, J. M. 1999. *Juran's Quality Handbook,* Fifth ed.
    Milwaukee: ASQ Quality Press.

Mills, C. A. 1988. *The Quality Audit: A Management
    Evaluation Tool.* McGraw-Hill Professional.

Parsowith, B. S. 1995. *Fundamentals of Quality Auditing.*
    Milwaukee: ASQC Quality Press.

Russell, J.P., and T. Regel. 2000. *After the Quality Audit:
    Closing the Loop on the Audit Process,* Second ed.
    Milwaukee: ASQ Quality Press.

Wilson, P. F., L. D. Dell, and G. F. Anderson. 1993. *Root
    Cause Analysis: A Tool for Total Quality Management.*
    Milwaukee: ASQC Quality Press.

SOCIETY REFERENCES

ASTD
American Society for Training and Development
1640 King Street, Box 1443
Alexandria, VA 22313-2043
www.astd.org
800-NAT-ASTD

ISPI
International Society for Performance
   Improvement
1400 Spring Street, Ste. 260
Silver Spring, MD 20910
www.ispi.org
301-587-8570

Index